Voices From Around the IEP Table

Voices From Around the IEP Table

Perspectives on Culturally and Linguistically Diverse Families

Karrin Lukacs
Sherry L. Steeley

ROWMAN & LITTLEFIELD
Lanham • Boulder • New York • London

Published by Rowman & Littlefield
An imprint of The Rowman & Littlefield Publishing Group, Inc.
4501 Forbes Boulevard, Suite 200, Lanham, Maryland 20706
www.rowman.com

Unit A, Whitacre Mews, 26-34 Stannary Street, London SE11 4AB

British Library Cataloguing in Publication Information Available

Library of Congress Cataloging-in-Publication Data

Names: Lukacs, Karrin, 1969– author. | Steeley, Sherry L., 1967– author.
Title: Voices from around the IEP table : perspectives on culturally and linguistically diverse families
     / Karrin Lukacs, Sherry L. Steeley.
Description: Lanham, MD : Rowman & Littlefield, [2018] | Includes bibliographical references.
Identifiers: LCCN 2018029422 (print) | LCCN 2018042914 (ebook) | ISBN 9781475841473 (elec-
     tronic) | ISBN 9781475841459 (cloth : alk. paper) | ISBN 9781475841466 (pbk. : alk. paper)
Subjects: LCSH: Individualized education programs. | Children with disabilities—Education. | Inter-
     cultural communication in education.
Classification: LCC LC4019 (ebook) | LCC LC4019 .L36 2018 (print) | DDC 371.39/4—dc23
LC record available at https://lccn.loc.gov/2018029422

Printed in the United States of America

To the three most important voices in my life—those of my children, Matilda and Michael B, and my husband, Michael.—K. L.

To my son Henry, whose voice educates, enlivens, and enlightens my perspectives on life and daily experiences.—S. L. S.

And to all those currently working for improvement in cultural and linguistic diversity and special education and enhanced prospects for students in U.S. schools.

Contents

Acknowledgments   ix

Introduction   xi

1   The Principal's Voice: "There are cultures of expectations."   1

2   The General Education Teacher's Voice: "Am I a good teacher?"   11

3   The Special Education Teacher's Voice: "It's not that complicated."   21

4   The ESOL Teacher's Voice: "Others just sit and watch . . . I get involved."   29

5   The Advocate's Voice: "There should be no hidden agendas— this is someone's life."   41

6   The Disability Rights Attorney's Voice: "It's emotionally and legally complex."   49

7   The Parent's Voice: "It is always embattled, you know?"   57

8   The Translator's Voice: "Translation is a moral responsibility."   67

9   The School Psychologist's Voice: "There are lots of pieces to think about."   77

10   The Specialist's Voice: "Everyone has to take a turn."   85

11   The Transition Services Specialist's Voice: "The buck stops here."   93

12   The Guidance Counselor's Voice: "I take the back door."   99

Conclusion   111

Appendix: Commonly Used Acronyms   119

References   121

About the Authors 125

Acknowledgments

Both Karrin and Sherry would like to acknowledge the support of Dr. David Brazer, associate professor of teaching and faculty director of Leadership Degree Programs at Stanford University. This book would not have been possible without him.

Karrin and Sherry would also like to acknowledge the many individuals who graciously shared their time and experiences. While they cannot be named for reasons of confidentiality, their assistance is truly appreciated.

Introduction

The world of special education can be a bewildering place. In an attempt to explain it, education professionals often share a particular metaphor. In this metaphor, parents are asked to imagine that they have been planning for a trip to Italy. In preparation, they have studied the culture and mapped out their itinerary. The flight goes smoothly, but when they disembark from the plane, they find themselves in Holland rather than in Italy—still Europe, but not at all what they had expected. The parents quickly discover that they are inadequately prepared for this trip, and as a result, frustration, anger, and confusion ensue, and it is often the case that they never fully acclimate to the situation.

It is easy to understand why people use this metaphor to describe what it is like to learn that a child has special needs. Now, take it one step further and imagine that all of the cultural resources they have studied and the travel books they read are written in a language that is not their native tongue. So in addition to not being where they expected to be, these parents in culturally and linguistically diverse families must also negotiate how to navigate this new trip in a language with which they are not comfortable. They experience the same frustration, anger, and confusion, and also the extra challenge of having to translate unfamiliar information into their native language.

This book is rooted in our professional and personal experiences as K–12 teachers and teacher educators, and as parents familiar with the special education system. One of us has worked in secondary English for Speakers of Other Languages (ESOL) teaching and had the experience of struggling to advocate for students who were culturally and linguistically diverse (CLD)[1] with special needs, before continuing on to study and work in teacher education. The other is a former K–6 general education teacher who worked in a highly diverse school district. Over 75% of the students were recent immigrants to the United States, and the majority of their parents had very little formal school experience in general and no experience with special education in particular.

As parents, in turn, we have also been engaged with public education and individualized education programs (IEPs) more than two decades. The experience has been daunting, even for two well-educated, native-English-speaking parents holding terminal degrees in the field of education. From an equity perspective, we believe that if we confronted challenges navigating the IEP process, those challenges must be all the more significant for parents from other cultural and linguistic backgrounds.

Extensive research documents the challenges confronting CLD parents as they navigate the special education process in public education. These challenges range from language barriers to insufficient information about the process, culturally rooted views of the roles of parents and teachers, and views of education that vary considerably from the norm in the American educational system. U.S. educators are often unaware of these invisible cultural barriers and may assume detachment or disinterest on the part of parents who may not understand their rights or who may be confused or overwhelmed by the process.

WHAT WE DECIDED TO DO

As a result, we undertook initial research interviews with CLD parents in various school districts to attempt to understand their experiences and perspectives. In our reading, we discovered a framework model developed by researchers in this field that yielded a guideline for best practices in working with CLD families involved in the special education process (Blue-Banning, Summers, Frankland, Nelson, & Beegle, 2004). We used this tool to explore CLD parents' perceptions of how well schools were serving their children's special education needs. If we were to express our approach graphically, it would resemble Figure 0.1.

After publishing a case study on the experiences of one family, and continuing our interviews, we began to think that we were encountering cultural differences theory in action (e.g., Good, Masewicz, & Vogel, 2010). In order to explore this further, we realized we needed to explore the viewpoints of other stakeholders involved in working on these issues, and so we developed the idea of using the IEP table itself to frame our investigation. Figure 0.2 reflects our modified approach.

This book is a result of that work. In it, we share the interviews with a number of stakeholders in the IEP process, including a school principal; general education, ESOL, and special education teachers; an educational advocate; a special education attorney; a family with a child receiving special

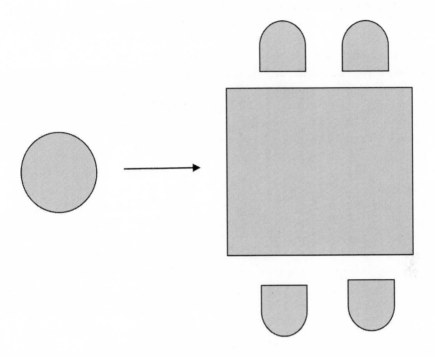

Figure 0.1. Conceptual Framework 1: Individual Perspective

education services; a family liaison/translator; a school psychologist; a specialist; a transition services specialist; and a guidance counselor. In order to better understand how we have structured this book, we want to share information about IEP meetings in general and our conceptual framework in particular.

IEP MEETINGS

IEP meetings are an opportunity for a team of individuals to review and/or to make recommendations regarding a student's annual progress toward meeting stated goals. The team members include the child's family, the principal (or designee), the school psychologist, a special education teacher, a general education teacher, and other interested individuals the school or the family would like to invite. [2]

During these meetings, the IEP team discusses the student's Present Level of Performance (PLOP), [3] annual goals, and her/his individualized supports and services. For the PLOP, the IEP team leader drafts a statement about the child's current levels of academic and functional performance and corre-

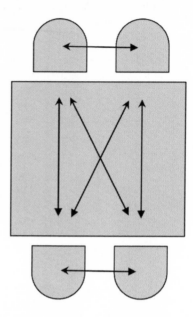

Figure 0.2.   Conceptual Framework 2: Multiple Perspectives

sponding goals. These goals are based on data such as test scores, anecdotal notes, and observations shared by the team members.

For the annual goals, the IEP team reviews the progress made by the student in terms of academic and functional performance. Based on the discussion of the data collected, the goals can be revised or new ones can be developed. These goals are meant to be specific and unique to the child rather than boilerplate statements.

For the individualized supports and services, the IEP team discusses what supports are needed to meet the child's academic and functional goals. These supports can include accommodations, modifications, and/or specialized instruction. The IEP team should ensure that these supports and services align with the PLOP and annual goals.

This is, of course, a simplified—and perhaps idealized—summary of what an IEP meeting looks like. It is often the case that each team member holds a different set of expectations with regard to the student and, as a result, there can be experiences of frustration, anger, and confusion—feelings that can be heightened when cultural and linguistic differences are also involved. In an attempt to make sense out of the many dynamics in play during an IEP meeting, we decided to adopt a conceptual framework to guide our interview sessions.

OUR CONCEPTUAL FRAMEWORK

Over the two years that we conducted interviews, we heard one phrase repeated over and over: "It's us versus them." While we might have expected to hear parents express this sentiment, we were surprised that nearly every school-based team member remarked on the seemingly inherent conflict embedded in the IEP meeting process. Given that we hoped to reduce the "us versus them" dynamic by presenting experiences and providing suggestions that emerged from team members' experiences, we turned to the work of Blue-Banning et al. (2004) to frame our interview questions. The six general themes we explored with each interviewee were communication, commitment, equality, skills, trust, and respect.[4]

1. Communication

In effective IEP meetings with CLD families, the quality of communication is positive, understandable, and respectful among all members at all levels of the partnership. The quality of communication is also at a level to enable efficient and effective coordination and understanding among all members. Indicators of communication include sharing resources, being clear, being honest, communicating positively, being tactful, being open, listening, communicating frequently, and coordinating information.

2. Commitment

The members of an effective IEP partnership share a sense of assurance about each other's devotion and loyalty to the child and family and each other's belief in the importance of the goals being pursued on behalf of the child and family. Indicators of commitment include demonstrating commitment, being flexible, regarding work as "more than a job," regarding the child and family as "more than a case," encouraging the child and family, being accessible to the child and family, being consistent, and being sensitive to emotions.

3. Equality

When equality is present, the members of an IEP meeting with a CLD family feel a sense of equity in decision making and service implementation and actively work to ensure that all other members of the partnership feel equally powerful in their ability to influence outcomes for children and families. Indicators of equality include avoiding use of "clout," empowering partners, validating others, advocating for the child or family with other professionals, being willing to explore all options, fostering harmony among all partners, avoiding "turfism," and acting "equal."

4. Skills

Members of the IEP meeting perceive that other team members have the necessary skills to be successful when others on the team demonstrate competence, including an ability to fulfill their roles and to exemplify "recommended practice" approaches to working with CLD children and families. Indicators of skills include taking action, having expectations for the child's progress, meeting individual special needs, considering the whole child or family, and being willing to learn.

5. Trust

If the members of the IEP team share a sense of assurance about the reliability or dependability of the character, capability, strength, or truth of the other members of the partnership, they report strong feelings of trust in the motives and decisions of their fellow team members. Indicators of trust include being reliable, keeping the child safe, and being discreet.

6. Respect

Perhaps the most important theme is that of respect. Defined as when the members of the IEP team regard each other with esteem and demonstrate that esteem through actions and communications, indicators of respect include valuing the child, being nonjudgmental, being courteous, exercising nondiscrimination, and avoiding intrusion.

HOW THIS BOOK IS ORGANIZED

Each chapter of this book focuses on the experiences of a stakeholder who is present at IEP meetings with CLD families. Each interviewee is a representative of someone in that role, but it is important to remember that their experiences might not represent the entire depth and breadth of all individuals who hold that particular position or title.

In Chapter 1, we meet Dr. Moudry,[5] a principal who discusses the need for improved communications and expectations among stakeholders, and for addressing challenging topics in order to improve the IEP process and educational outcomes.

In Chapter 2, we meet Ms. Klog, a general education teacher who talks about the difficult choices she must make—and the pressure she feels from her in-school colleagues—when trying to advocate for CLD students.

In Chapter 3, we meet Ms. Matalino, a special education teacher who, as a fluent Spanish speaker, often finds herself walking a fine line between assisting the parents and representing the school's interests.

In Chapter 4, we meet Ms. Hekima, an ESOL teacher who is passionately invested in ensuring that the families of her students understand their rights and learn to advocate for their children, lest school districts funnel them through a preordained pipeline.

In Chapter 5, we meet Ms. Amamihe, a special education advocate who outlines areas that schools should address in order to overcome an "us versus them" dynamic.

In Chapter 6, we meet Ms. Ologbon, a disability rights attorney who focuses her concerns on individualizing school district approaches to children and following due process in providing the services as codified by the IEP.

In chapter 7, we meet Ms. Tark, a parent who has undertaken extensive education in order to maximize opportunities for her son within the parameters of a least restrictive environment and available services.

In Chapter 8, we meet Ms. Bolcs, a translator who often finds herself trying to negotiate the relationship(s) between translation, interpretation, and advocacy.

In Chapter 9, we meet Ms. Wijaksana, a school psychologist who stresses the importance of clear and consistent communication among and between IEP team members.

In Chapter 10, we meet Ms. Donos, a specialist[6] who feels that schools should do a better job of ensuring that general education teachers have ample and equal opportunities to work with CLD students.

In Chapter 11, we meet Dr. Bulumko, a transition services specialist who sees himself as the "bridge" between a student's school and postsecondary worlds. Mr. Bulumko is also the person who must inject realistic expectations—sometimes for the first time—into the IEP meeting process.

In chapter 12, we meet Ms. Cialmhar, a guidance counselor who is willing to subvert the system in order to make sure that CLD students who receive special education services get equitable treatment in schools.

In our conclusion, we summarize and analyze the key takeaways from our conversations with the stakeholders and revisit the conceptual framework discussed earlier.

As you read, you will no doubt notice that there are similarities across the stakeholders' experiences and their suggestions for improvement. These are noted as appropriate in each chapter. While some points may feel redundant, we believe that this "overlap" adds weight and validity to the themes that emerge, all of which we explore further in the conclusion.

Our goal is for this book to encourage challenging conversations. As such, at the end of each chapter, we provide additional articles, books, reports, and/or websites for further exploration, as well as questions for reflection and discussion. It is our fervent hope that furthering such discussions among stakeholders will continue to further progress for all students, so that the educational process will enable them to maximize their potential for full participation in national civic and economic life.

NOTES

1. We believe strongly in the importance of person-first language, as we have written here. However, for the sake of clarity, subsequent references to this population will be label-first (i.e., CLD students).

2. Starting at age 14, the child may also attend.

3. Examples of items that might be included on the PLOP are evaluation results; a list of the child's after-school activities, hobbies, and interests; descriptions of academic achievement and social or physical development; and management needs.

4. Although we feel that these themes do a good job of capturing the perspectives of the IEP team members, we encourage readers to develop alternative ideas or perspectives that focus attention and thinking on how to work more collaboratively and improve students' performance.

5. The observant reader will note that each pseudonym is the word "wise" in a language other than English.

6. There are many specialists in a school building who might participate in an IEP meeting. For this book, we chose a speech/language pathologist (S/LP) because many CLD students are often first referred for special education services due to a delay in expressive speech.

Chapter One

The Principal's Voice

"There are cultures of expectations."

In Individualized Education Program (IEP) meetings, a principal or principal-designee provides leadership and ensures the participation of the IEP team members, which includes parents, special and general education teachers, and any specialists involved. Formally, the principal represents the school district, providing oversight of special education services and resources. In order to be successful in this role, the principal must be very familiar with the range of available services, district special education policy, and the general education curriculum (McElhinny & Pellegrin, 2014). Ideally, the principal should provide leadership as an honest broker among the stakeholders.

The principal we interviewed, Dr. Moudry, brings to his position a doctorate in educational leadership as well as several years of experience as a school administrator. He is relatively new in his position as a high school principal, but previously held two assistant principal posts and has more than a decade of English for Speakers of Other Languages (ESOL) teaching experience in public education.

Due to his work with ESOL students in a very diverse district, he is familiar with the needs of various populations, issues of inclusion, and culturally responsive schools. As a member of a traditionally underrepresented population and a former military officer, Dr. Moudry's personal and professional experiences inform his perspectives on equity for all students across economic, cultural, and linguistic lines.

Over the years, Dr. Moudry has participated in numerous IEP meetings and has broad observations on culture, dynamics, emotions, and outcomes. While as a new principal he has thus far presided over relatively few meet-

1

ings involving culturally and linguistically diverse (CLD) students and their families, his prior work in public education as an ESOL teacher positions him to offer numerous insights. His perspectives focus particularly on the dynamics of IEP meetings and the role of teachers. His views in turn suggest pathways to improving the process and outcomes for CLD students and families.

PERSPECTIVES ON CULTURAL AND LINGUISTIC DIVERSITY

Due to his years of working with CLD students and families in his capacity as an ESOL teacher prior to entering administration, Dr. Moudry's perspectives are informed by his experiences. He views cultural background as the single most significant determinant of how parents interact with the school.

Cultural and Class Differences

Overall, Dr. Moudry believes that CLD families tend to trust the school. Researchers (and the people we interviewed for this book) recount that in many other cultures, parents view school authorities with enormous respect and defer to their expertise. This may signal acceptance of the reports that experts and teachers are sharing. Dr. Moudry reports that, in his experience with CLD parents, they are often reticent about asking questions lest they appear doubtful about or ungrateful for the education their children are receiving.

While he notes that the school's parent liaison or translator may encourage parents to ask questions, meetings with CLD parents who lack a strong education typically do not last long. Even well-educated parents may lack an understanding of special education services and often respond by saying that they don't know what to say when asked for their input. School personnel may expect that parents know what is going on, and look askance at what they view as a lack of preparation or interest rather than a cultural difference when no questions are forthcoming.

Ultimately, Dr. Moudry believes that CLD families tend to trust the system, tend to be overwhelmed in meetings, and then tend to put the IEP away after the meeting and not look at it again for another year.

The converse is true for majority-culture parents, particularly those with experience, education, and an understanding of school and district dynamics. Dr. Moudry's experience has led him to believe that socioeconomic class is much more important than race or cultural background. Parents who are affluent understand that the IEP is a legal document and hire advocates to attend meetings to ensure the best possible IEP outcome for their children. He believes that this is most evident in the testing accommodations that their children receive. Ultimately, he says, "Parents who know what IEP they want usually get the IEP they want."

Impact on Teachers

Administrators have expectations of both parents and teachers. Many expect the teachers to come prepared with data in order to address future goal setting and academic performance. Teachers are often wedded to their approaches and expect to continue their approaches, resisting change. Teachers expect that parents will fall into the category of passive parents, supportive parents, or "crazy" (overdemanding or oppositional) parents, and react accordingly. Ironically, each type of parent, for different reasons, reinforces teachers' preexisting views that their approaches do not need to change.

PERSPECTIVES ON THE IEP MEETING

Dr. Moudry's professional experiences also include being a part of IEP teams for CLD students. He believes that there are several key factors to consider when trying to ensure that the meeting is a success: being organized, communicating effectively, managing contention, and supporting teachers.

Organization

In Dr. Moudry's experience, successful IEP meetings are rooted in respect and equity from the outset of the planning process. The best IEP meetings are set up at the convenience of parents, take place in an adequate meeting room, and start on time. As Dr. Moudry states, "Just because parents are not present doesn't mean they don't care." However, many parents do not have flexible work hours, and scheduling should focus on their needs since they are key participants.

In Dr. Moudry's view, the leader of the meeting should explain the process and agenda of the meeting and give everyone assurance that they will have the chance to talk. The principal should always remind everyone of the reason they are present: to benefit the student. Only then should the meeting move to the psychologist's report, teacher narratives, and parent input. Team members should establish IEP goals collaboratively based on data from student performance.

Dr. Moudry acknowledges that IEP meetings can occur under far less favorable conditions. A poorly managed IEP meeting can disregard the parents' schedules, with school officials merely informing the parents when the meeting will be held. Meetings may be rushed or start late. In so doing, the school sends a message that they are in charge and, perhaps inadvertently, that parent needs and input are secondary.

In these cases, parents may be unable to attend or to contribute adequately and may begin the process with a sense of being diminished or disrespected. Essentially, this establishes a power imbalance at the outset. These are problems also highlighted by other interviewees, including the general education teacher (Chapter 2), the special education teacher (Chapter 3), the ESOL teacher (Chapter 4), and the translator (Chapter 8).

Communication

In addition to focusing everyone on the purpose of the meeting—to support the student—Dr. Moudry believes that it is important to ensure from the outset that everyone speaks with the student in mind and that the principal keeps student interests at the forefront. A bad IEP meeting will commence with staff sending papers around the table for signature, taking time to set up the technology, and other bureaucratic tasks, before launching into a litany of reporting and "judgments" about the students.

Reporting may be full of technical terminology or "psychobabble" that is incomprehensible to parents. Dr. Moudry believes that psychologists are the worst offenders when it comes to using jargon, presenting their information without taking questions, and becoming defensive when there are questions from the group.

When the experts are running through their presentations, language matters. Even for parents whose native language is English, the technical language of special education may be somewhat incomprehensible and can be rendered even more opaque by the use of acronyms[1] for service categories and specialists. Mere translation does not convey the significance of the information or its implications. While this is likely driven by interaction with other professionals, Dr. Moudry believes it is very important that this be communicated instead in clear English that can be readily translated. Test scores should be explained, as should the instructional methods.

Other factors can undermine meeting dynamics as well. The department chair may attempt to "march through an IEP meeting with predetermined outcomes." He or she may run quickly through the meeting, fail to offer options or explain services, or otherwise seem unwelcoming or negative. When this happens, parents and students can be forgotten. In a good IEP meeting, CLD parents are encouraged to speak with open time for their input.

Dr. Moudry, along with the advocate (Chapter 5), the translator (Chapter 8), and the guidance counselor (Chapter 12), stresses the importance of clear communication and knowledgeable translation. Too often, however, there is merely a perfunctory, "Do you have any questions?" after a long presentation by teachers and specialists. As principal, Dr. Moudry attempts always to steer the conversation back to the parents and to the larger purpose of the meeting.

Contention

In Dr. Moudry's experience, sometimes an IEP meeting can be derailed by interpersonal dynamics. If the school representatives rush through a meeting, if CLD parents are kept waiting without an apology, or if teachers focus on the negative aspects of the child's behavior, emotions can run high and interpersonal dynamics can become contentious. Parents become suspicious of the motives of the principal and the other IEP team members, and those feelings of mistrust can be mutual. These interactions often lead to avoidance of important issues in an effort to keep the tone of the meeting pleasant and nonconfrontational. As Dr. Moudry puts it, "We shy away from difficult conversations."

As a result, when school officials anticipate a difficult IEP meeting, they often conduct a "meeting before the meeting" in which they agree on their approach and what the IEP will look like. They then present a united front to CLD parents with little conceptual space for parent input. While the principal and the school representatives might feel that they are doing the parents a favor by shortening the time spent in the meeting, parents often feel rushed, ignored, or overlooked.

In an effort to provide balance between CLD parents and the school, some districts have an official in the central office who attends IEP meetings to serve as a neutral liaison between the two. This person does not take the place of a parent's advocate, but is there to ensure an IEP that is fair to all parties.

If CLD parents have an advocate, that advocate may negotiate directly with this district representative. Otherwise, the representative may tend to protect parent interests, particularly if no one else at the table seems to be doing so. In Dr. Moudry's experience, this can create a volatile situation. When the liaison is at odds with the school, staff feel betrayed and defensive, and relationships among the parties at the table can become poisoned. This may undermine trust, not just in the meeting in progress, but in all future meetings. The process may become more about "winning" than what is best for the student, and emotions can become overwhelming.

Dr. Moudry has found, however, that tears—on the part of parents or teachers—are a great humanizer. At a contentious meeting, everyone backs down when tears are shed; at a noncontentious meeting, everyone feels validated by them. In other words, tears demonstrate the depth of commitment to the student, the personal involvement in education, the frustration with limits, and the need for progress. They often emanate from conflict, but dissipate tension and remind everyone of the purpose of the meeting at its foundation: the best interests for education of the student.

As you will see, many others discuss these dynamics, including the general education teacher (Chapter 2), the special education teacher (Chapter 3), the ESOL teacher (Chapter 4), the advocate (Chapter 5), the parent (Chapter 7), the translator (Chapter 8), and the guidance counselor (Chapter 12).

Teachers

When hiring special education teachers, Dr. Moudry looks for people with a "heart for kids," people who—in addition to holding the appropriate education requirements—have been involved in scouts, camp counseling, or other community activities that support children's development. He firmly believes that "Kids work for the teacher, not for the grade," and that this is especially true for children with special needs.

As a former teacher, Dr. Moudry believes strongly that teachers are doing their best for CLD students with IEPs. That said, he is similarly convinced by his experience that the case manager should *not* be a teacher because the goals that result are much stronger when someone else is in charge of the student's development. His belief emerges from several related factors. First, he says that teachers are very rooted in the moment, in their teaching, and in the dynamics of the meeting, and that as a result, they struggle to write goals for an annual plan. Seeing a student day in and day out means that they can recall and think about successes and failures in the present and recent past, but are less able to conceptualize larger goals.

Next, he noted that teachers, because they are on the front lines, are very attached to their programs and their approaches. Many resist and dislike change. Finally, he said, because the teachers want the goals to be attainable, the goals are likely to be less rigorous than when written by someone without the same daily experiences with the students. They do not want to fail their students and do not want to fail themselves, and as a result, set goals that may be more imminently achievable than someone focused on a target for a year in the future.

On a broader note, Dr. Moudry has seen many IEP meetings in which teachers themselves do not really understand the complexity of some of the IEP language. As can be the case for CLD parents, some of the jargon is simply incomprehensible. "All they know is that the IEP meeting is taking a long time," he said.

An additional problem for teachers, Dr. Moudry believes, lies in teachers' uneasy relationship with data. Data collection and interpretation skills should be added to licensure requirements or provided as professional development so that teachers know how to collect useful data on student performance, how to use this information in the classroom, and how to let it drive goal setting in IEP meetings. Exacerbating this problem is that too often, teachers are excluded from dialogues about data that occur among specialists. This is also a problem for CLD parents who rely almost exclusively on the data reported quarterly by teachers to understand progress toward IEP goals. In subsequent chapters, others also discuss various areas of special education training for teachers, as reflected in the perspectives of the general education teacher (Chapter 2), the ESOL teacher (Chapter 4), and the specialist (Chapter 10).

SUGGESTIONS FOR IMPROVEMENT

When asked for his suggestions on how to improve IEP meetings with CLD students and their families, Dr. Moudry has several ideas. These include making changes to the structure of the meeting itself, being sure to communicate clearly, and training teachers to collect data.

IEP Meeting Dynamics

As Dr. Moudry noted, there are features of a "good" IEP meeting that cannot be taken for granted and should be foundational standard practice. Basic courtesies in planning IEP meetings ensure everyone's comfort and participation. Schools and parents should establish mutually convenient meeting times, and the meetings should start on time. Meeting locations should be spacious enough for all participants. Meetings should commence with introductions and establish clearly that everyone will have the chance to talk. Parents should be encouraged to ask questions *during* presentations by psychologists, case managers, and teachers' reports on progress, and then given a clear participatory role in developing goals and measures.

Ensure Transparency of Language

Because families from CLD backgrounds may be less familiar with the culture of special education, translators seem to play an outsized role in determining parental input. Translating the technical language of an IEP meeting literally does not necessarily ensure understanding; even native speakers are sometimes unaware of the implications of particular phraseology or the importance of the wording of goals or levels of performance, specialized acronyms or offices, or the nature of services to be delivered. The translators themselves, without additional background, may be unable to fully explain specialized jargon regardless of language proficiency.

In numerous interviews, we've heard that there has been a dynamic of specialists requesting only literal translation of their words. Bilingual teachers report that their attempts to explain concepts to parents have been halted, even when parents do not comprehend the meaning of the technical explanations. As such, it is understandable that interpretation by nonspecialists could result in misunderstandings.

In this light, Dr. Moudry suggests that a better approach might involve two levels of training—one for specialists and one for translators. Specialists could be trained in using simple English so that everyone around the table can understand. The "Plain English movement"—which emerged in the 1970s to simplify government, business, and legal language—might offer an appropriate framework for accomplishing this. Using Plain English guidelines, meetings could be free of jargon, acronyms, and unnecessarily complex references with technical language presented in clear terms.

Translators, in turn, could receive district or state-provided training on the IEP process, special education eligibility and services, and reporting, data, and other tools for communication. This would enable them to provide accurate explanations to CLD parents throughout the process, not merely during the IEP meeting itself.

Ideally, both plain language and translation could become hallmarks of the IEP meeting process, with supporting documents communicated clearly to CLD and native speakers alike. This would primarily entail editing writing style to ensure that sentences are short and technical terms are explained, and applying these principles to IEP meeting discussions. Doing so would improve comprehension and participation not just for parents, but for teachers, advocates, and others with a voice at the table.

Emphasize Data Collection and Data-Driven Decision Making

As Dr. Moudry notes, teachers should come to IEP meetings with data corresponding to goals as written, in order to evaluate progress and establish goals that represent appropriate steps forward for the coming year. He believes that doing so would also help teachers focus on goals on a regular basis, set higher expectations, and align instruction with identified learning needs. The IEP team could then discuss the data with teachers in order to identify specifics on areas for future instructional focus. Too often, evidence presented in meetings is anecdotal or based on hunches.

In order to better prepare teachers, training on the use of data in the instructional cycle generally—with direct application to the special education instructional cycle—is critical. Data should drive instruction, which in turn generates additional data. This is not intuitive, however; instead, it relies on improved training for those who are working most closely with students.

Currently, many teachers are uncomfortable with data, and this impedes a well-grounded planning process and perhaps in some cases leaves teachers at a loss in meetings. Because CLD parents rely on the same data reported quarterly, the parties closest to the students are then less than ideally positioned to develop goals and objectives for subsequent planning cycles.

QUESTIONS FOR DISCUSSION/REFLECTION

- How important is the principal's role in the IEP meetings for CLD students? How does a principal's position shape his or her perspectives on the process?
- Dr. Moudry comments that students "work for the teacher, not the grade." How true is this in your experience?
- Why does a power imbalance seem to characterize some IEP meetings? Assuming that everyone is well-intentioned, what are some ways a principal might bridge this divide?
- Given the fact that special education is a field with very technical language involved, how can a principal improve communications in meetings?
- Dr. Moudry advocates for the use of Plain English. Do you think this is a viable approach? Why or why not?
- Do you think that most principals would agree that translators should receive specialized training so that they can explain the ideas they are translating? Why or why not?
- Do you agree with Dr. Moudry that further training in data collection and analysis would be helpful for special education teachers? If so, what kinds of training would most benefit teachers to facilitate their work with data? Should it be part of the licensure process? In a workshop or online format? Or should specialists assist them in these tasks?

NOTE

1. See the appendix for a list of commonly used acronyms in IEP meetings.

ADDITIONAL RESOURCES

These articles, books, reports, and/or websites provide more information about the topics mentioned in this chapter.

Cultural Differences

Berman, P., Aburto, S., Nelson, B., Minicucci, C., & Burkart, G. (2000). *Going schoolwide: Comprehensive school reform inclusive of limited English proficient students.* Washington, DC: Office of Bilingual Education and Minority Language Affairs. Retrieved from http://www.ncela.us/files/rcd/BE020926/Going_Schoolwide_Comprehensive.pdf

Borman, K. M., Fox, A. E., & Levinson, B. A. U. (2000). Cultural production and reproduction in contemporary schools. In B. Levinson (Ed.), *Schooling the symbolic animal: Social and cultural dimensions of education* (pp. 239–247). New York: Rowman & Littlefield.

Brooks, K., Adams, S. R., & Morita-Mullaney, T. (2010). Creating inclusive learning communities for ELL students: transforming school principals' perspectives. *Theory into Practice, 49*, 145–151. https://doi.org/10.1080/00405841003641501

Bruner, J. (1996). *The culture of education.* Cambridge, MA: Harvard University Press.
Cummins, J. (2000). *Language, power, and pedagogy: Bilingual children in the crossfire.* Buffalo, NY: Multilingual Matters, Ltd.
Leake, D., & Black, R. (2005). *Essential tools: Cultural and linguistic diversity: Implications for transition personnel.* Minneapolis: University of Minnesota, Institute on Community Integration, National Center on Secondary Education and Transition. Retrieved from http://www.ncset.org/publications/essentialtools/diversity/partIV.asp

Data-Driven Instruction

Gordillo, W. J., & Miller, A. (2017). Progress monitoring with data collection of IEP annual goals. Boston: Public Consulting Group Inc. Retrieved from http://www.publicconsultinggroup.com/education/library/white_papers/EDU_OFCL_White_Paper_PMDC%20Final.pdf
Halverson, R., Grigg, J., Prichett, R., & Thomas, C. (2006). *The new instructional leadership: Creating data-driven instructional systems in schools.* Retrieved from https://www.researchgate.net/profile/Richard_Halverson/publication/228363590_The_new_instruction_leadership_Creating_data-driven_instructional_systems_in_schools/links/0c960531126ac25e67000000.pdf
New Jersey Department of Education (2015–2016). Utilizing data to inform instruction (LRE Training Module, New Jersey Department of Education). Retrieved fromhttp://www.state.nj.us/education/specialed/idea/lre/year1trainings/2/UtilizingDatatoInformInstruction.pdf
Wakeman, S., & Henderson, K. (2012). Data collection: An introduction—A facilitator's guide for professional development. Modules Addressing Special Education and Teacher Education (MAST), East Carolina University. Retrieved from http://mast.ecu.edu/modules/dbd/lib/documents/FG-Wakeman-Data%20Collection.pdf
Wakeman, S., & Henderson, K. (2012). Data collection: An introduction—A PowerPoint presentation for professional development. Modules Addressing Special Education and Teacher Education (MAST), East Carolina University. Retrieved from http://mast.ecu.edu/modules/dbd/lib/documents/PPT-Wakeman-Data%20Collection.pdf
Webster, J. (2017). *Data collection for individual education plan implementation.* New York: ThoughtCo. Retrieved from https://www.thoughtco.com/data-collection-for-iep-implementation-3110992

Language

Hart, J. E., Cheatham, G., & Jimenez-Silva, M. (2012). Facilitating quality language interpretation for families of diverse students with special needs. *Preventing School Failure, 56*(4), 207–213.
Top 10 Principles for Plain Language: https://www.archives.gov/open/plain-writing/10-principles.html
U.S. Department of Education Plain Writing Initiative: https://www.ed.gov/plain-language

Parent Participation

Doblowski, D. M. (2004). Encouraging active parent participation in IEP team meetings. *Teaching Exceptional Children, 36*(3), 34–39.
Lo, L. (2012). Demystifying the IEP process for diverse parents of children with disabilities. *Teaching Exceptional Children, 44*(3), 14–20.
Wolfe, K., & Duran, L. K. (2013) Culturally and linguistically diverse parents' perceptions of the IEP process. *Multiple Voices for Ethnically Diverse Exceptional Learners, 13*(2), 4–18.
Zhang, C., & Bennett, T. (2003). Facilitating the meaningful participation of culturally and linguistically diverse families in the IFSP and IEP process. *Focus on Autism and Other Developmental Disabilities, 18*(1), 51–59.

Chapter Two

The General Education Teacher's Voice

"Am I a good teacher?"

Every Individualized Education Program (IEP) meeting must include a general education teacher. While she does not design the instruction supporting IEP goals, she does support the instructional efforts of the special education teacher. Perhaps more importantly, she is a rich source of data about the degree to which special education instruction is impacting a student's performance in a general setting when the special education teacher is not present. She can speak generally to a student's social and academic interactions, his strengths and challenges, and issues and areas of need that emerge during the day-to-day interactions and observations of the student.

The general education teacher we interviewed, Ms. Klog, is a career switcher with five years of experience as an elementary education teacher. Her previous professional experiences include work in health—first as a dietician and then, after several years as a stay-at-home mom, as an administrator for a large-scale corporate health savings account program. When she volunteered as a parent in her children's schools, people, seeing her aptitude at dealing with students, often asked her why she was not a teacher.

After considering the possibilities, she entered an online competency-based teacher education program that required extensive fieldwork and observations prior to a year of student teaching. Ms. Klog feels that the program prepared her well for the classroom, although there was not as much instruction on cultural diversity as she would have found useful for her work in a small but highly diverse school district. She describes herself as a passionate teacher who ensures that she knows her students and their parents.

As a parent, Ms. Klog had firsthand experience with the IEP process because one of her sons required an IEP. She said that even as an English-speaking parent with two degrees, she did not understand the purpose of the meeting, found the process confusing, and was not sure whether she was treated correctly. She was told to "just sign this," and was unaware of the implications of doing so.

PERSPECTIVES ON CULTURAL AND LINGUISTIC DIVERSITY

During her time as an elementary school teacher, Ms. Klog has participated in numerous referral, eligibility, and IEP meetings and has had a variety of experiences with teachers, specialists, parents, translators, and advocates. Currently, Ms. Klog works in a school that has a minority population of 85%, a large proportion of whom identify as Hispanic. As a result, she has developed insights into the dynamics among culturally and linguistically diverse (CLD) families and the special education process.

Cultural Outreach—School to Home

Ms. Klog believes there is a strong commitment to working with parents as partners, both in her highly diverse district and school. There are numerous activities scheduled on evenings and weekends, and teacher conferences occur on staggered schedules to accommodate a wide array of work schedules. Ms. Klog works hard to ensure that CLD parents—very few of whom are middle class—attend conferences. She believes this is valuable to enhance her understanding of a student's life experiences and for parents to understand their children's school experiences, achievements, and challenges.

Although she notes, "Sometimes parents don't have the best parenting practices," or that they may be limited in their contact time with their children due to holding multiple jobs, Ms. Klog believes that parent-teacher relationships are critical to supporting CLD students' education. Moreover, establishing these relationships early ensures that if a subsequent special education referral process occurs, communications are more likely to remain open.

The Referral Process for CLD Students

Because Ms. Klog teaches kindergarten, students rarely come to school with an IEP from their preschool years. "Most kids walk in as a blank slate," she notes. Thus, the first of her perspectives on IEP dynamics for CLD parents and families relates to the referral process. While four or five middle-class parents per year may initiate a referral for evaluation of their children for special education services, most evaluations for CLD or economically disadvantaged students are initiated by teachers.

She has learned, however, that because she is a general education teacher, she "has to pick her battles," and in light of the huge amount of data collection required and low probability of success, she initiates only a few per year. Put another way, since the burden of proof lies with her and/or the parents, she must choose students for whom they can make a good case.

When she thinks that a referral may be in order, Ms. Klog's first step is to meet with the parents. In these meetings, she can encounter parent resistance. Many parents of her CLD students are struggling to make ends meet and lack information. For this reason, they may fear the process or think that the school sees something wrong with their child.

If, after she explains the needs she has observed, the parents are amenable to proceeding with the Child Study process, [1] Ms. Klog often finds that the parents need the assistance of someone who can provide guidance because she has encountered the reality that the parents who push the hardest are the ones who obtain services. In other words, Ms. Klog often feels that children whose parents do suspect that something is wrong, but take no action, can slip through the cracks. She finds this to be especially true when working with CLD families, who are often reluctant to "make waves."

When Ms. Klog initiates a referral for a CLD student, she encounters numerous barriers. It is often the case that the first response of the school system is to dismiss her observations as a language, cultural, or behavioral issue. To Ms. Klog, this not only implies that she is doing something wrong in her classroom, but also a belief that the children need to adapt to American culture and learn English.

Prior to an official diagnosis, special education teachers do not participate in Child Study meetings, which means that Ms. Klog's is the only instructional perspective considered. During the first several meetings with the Child Study team, she is asked to demonstrate that the issues she has observed are not merely cultural or linguistic or a behavioral problem resulting from her own teaching methods. As such, Ms. Klog first receives recommendations for teaching practices to try in her classroom.

After that, there is an eight-week process of "remediation." During this time, she must collect data on the impact of the alternative practices she has tried in order to demonstrate that there is an underlying issue and that it is not her classroom methods that are causing poor behavior or performance. She feels that this puts teachers under a microscope, causing them to ask themselves if they are good teachers.

If a student is deemed to have a behavioral problem, school counselors are involved and counseling is sometimes recommended. If it is behavioral, she also must exhaust all options for alternative classroom arrangements prior to an evaluation and arrange for numerous observations by a diagnostician. If it is an academic problem, there is a push for improved English-language services and instructional techniques.

Due to the time-consuming nature of the Child Study process, Ms. Klog tends to focus on CLD students with the most obvious disabilities so that she has a better chance of obtaining services for them. This means that other students may fall by the wayside until their problems present greater academic challenges in later grades. Ms. Klog is frustrated by this dynamic, believing that the evaluation team, by default, assumes that students' issues and challenges are the teacher's fault.

PERSPECTIVES ON THE IEP MEETING

Ms. Klog's perspectives on IEP meetings focus almost entirely on meeting dynamics. Because parents usually do not understand the system, she attempts to discuss the process with them prior to the meeting. She believes strongly that parents need someone in the school who is on their side because otherwise, it is easy to attribute educational issues to linguistic problems rather than learning differences that result from developmental or disability-related challenges.

IEP Meeting Dynamics

Because administrators attend eligibility meetings as well as subsequent IEP meetings, they are the only consistent observers of both pre- and posteligibility determination besides the general education teacher. This is important, because the experiences of school officials with families make a difference in the services that a student receives. Ms. Klog has frequently observed that, if a parent is pushing hard for services, his child will receive better services.

Perceptions of other children in the family also have an impact, whether positive or negative. A view may be shared among school personnel that the sibling of a problem student will share similar issues. As Ms. Klog suggests, "Oh, another one in that family. We know what that's going to be." Further, she believes that, like most districts, hers tries to avoid adding a student to the special education rolls due to ever-contracting resource availability.

The dynamics Ms. Klog has observed for white, middle-class families and CLD families are dramatically different. White families initiate requests for and insist on services, she says, while CLD families receive what is offered. "If you don't speak English or don't have a law degree," she adds, "you're in trouble." White families often come in "with both barrels loaded" and the IEP team accedes to their demands, while CLD families come in as "deer in the headlights," and the team resists their input.

In the case of CLD families, Ms. Klog has noticed that there is also a greater attempt to refer families to services outside the school, while some in-school options or services are not offered or mentioned. Although her school views partnership with parents as crucial to student success in general, this view of partnership does not always make it into the IEP meeting room. As noted in the chapter on the principal (Chapter 1), this perspective is shared by many participants including the special education teacher (Chapter 3), the ESOL teacher (Chapter 4), the advocate (Chapter 5), the parent (Chapter 7), the translator (Chapter 8), the school psychologist (Chapter 9), and the guidance counselor (Chapter 12).

Language and Communication

In Ms. Klog's experience, although some school staff are bilingual, meetings tend to rely on formal translators and school personnel tend to stick to English. Meetings are conducted in very formal legal language, with translators often reading the documents aloud but translating only the formal language. Although some can interpret the language and summarize for parents using "normal" language, in many cases, Ms. Klog herself asks for a translation from "educationese" to the vernacular so that when translated into the family's native language, the meaning is more likely to be comprehensible to parents.

It is not uncommon for school personnel to talk among themselves in English, point to papers, and discuss process and modifications during the meeting. These conversations are seldom translated, so parents are in the dark and rarely stop the meeting to ask what is being discussed. When an advocate or lawyer is present, however, communication is much more extensively shared and much clearer. This dynamic also emerged in discussions with the principal (Chapter 1), the ESOL teacher (Chapter 4), the translator (Chapter 8), and the guidance counselor (Chapter 12).

The Teacher as Advocate

During an IEP meeting with a CLD family, Ms. Klog always sits next to the parents, not across from them, to convey to them that she is on the side of their child. As mentioned earlier, because parents are often totally overwhelmed, she regularly asks questions to clarify the meaning or implications of IEP process language and other terminology. Ms. Klog believes strongly that parents have to be the ones who choose what is right for their children, even when there is a "meeting before the meeting" in which school-based personnel predetermine what the IEP should contain.

In sum, Ms. Klog believes that CLD parents do not receive as much information as English-speaking families and that they understand less of what they should expect or request. Unfortunately, CLD families do not always realize that they are being treated unfairly in these circumstances. As a result of her advocacy, Ms. Klog said that she never goes into a meeting feeling like she's not "in the hot seat" and under intense scrutiny from the other school-based personnel.

School Strengths and Challenges

In spite of sometimes difficult dynamics, Ms. Klog believes that school personnel and specialists are well-trained, highly skilled, and committed to students. In many cases, however, teachers do not feel respected and esteemed as partners in the IEP process.

One problem is that they are simply stretched too thin. The speech and language pathologist at Ms. Klog's school, for example, is assigned to three schools and, as such, is not fully familiar with the staff and students at any of the three. This also makes getting a student onto the caseload of any such specialist very difficult.

An additional challenge is that there are few veteran teachers. While newer teachers may be more enthusiastic and less jaded than those with more experience, they often lack the perspectives or effective approaches that teaching experience brings.

SUGGESTIONS FOR IMPROVEMENT

Based on her experiences, Ms. Klog has numerous ideas for how to improve the special education process for CLD students. These focus on school resources in the area of instruction, training, and support for IEP meetings. While these resources are in short supply as school budgets continue to shrink in many jurisdictions, the ideas behind them are important to highlight as a way to stimulate thinking about creative approaches to IEP meetings.

Provide Training for General Education Teachers

From Ms. Klog's perspective, general education teachers need training on how to implement accommodations and on how to take data on student progress toward IEP goals. Throughout the evaluation process, she explained, she was reacting to recommendations for accommodations that she had not been trained to implement and had to do so without the help of a special education teacher because no IEP was yet in place.

Even after students receive an IEP with goals and accommodations outlined, the burden on general education teachers to implement them is not insignificant. While special education teachers take the lead and share methods and approaches with general education teachers, the increasing scarcity of resources means that to realize student potential in a general education setting, all teachers should be able to reinforce special education supports in the classrooms. With training in these measures, Ms. Klog thinks she would be much better positioned to do so.

Moreover, during the eligibility evaluation process, Ms. Klog must collect data on the impact of recommended accommodations but does not have the training to do so. Failing to assess or evaluate students in a way that can satisfy the requirements of eligibility determination potentially delays or derails a student's access to special education services. Providing training to her and other general education teachers would provide the additional benefit of allowing them to contribute to IEP data reporting by aligning collection practices with those of the special education teacher. This could potentially provide a fuller picture of student progress, most notably in a general education setting.

Allow Opportunities for Collaboration

Ms. Klog noted that while there are well-trained staff providing special education services, she has not observed enthusiasm or passion for the students they serve. This may be partially due to a feeling that scarce resources result in instructional staff being spread too thin, a lack of time to get to know students and their families, and a lack of joint planning time among special education, general education, and ESOL teachers. It is difficult to manage or recommend solutions for a lack of energy or enthusiasm, but mitigating conditions that may lead to cynicism and burnout could provide a pathway to improving the lives and professional energy of educational personnel.

In terms of collaboration, Ms. Klog suggested the possibility of implementing alternative scheduling to creatively engineer some joint planning and meeting time. If coupled with additional training, she feels that this could result in more creative thinking and coordination among teams of teachers working together for a common group of students.

Further, Ms. Klog feels that groups could focus on examining student performance and developing strategies to try to improve outcomes, to learn more about particular issues, and to provide important morale-enhancing support and motivation. In addition, she suggests that cross-disciplinary collaboration among special education teachers and others could also be beneficial (Grafwallner, 2017). Other strategies for professional learning groups recommended by experts include developing professional learning communities and voluntary issue groups (Caskey & Carpenter, 2014), and encouraging teachers to seek advice and to observe other teachers working in similar settings (Johnson, 2011).

Revise Meeting Dynamics

In Ms. Klog's view, meeting dynamics seem stacked against CLD families, particularly those without a high level of English-language skill and education. Bolstering the role of the translator is one step that she believes could help to remediate this gap. Designating a dedicated translator who would work across meetings would stimulate better conversations, as he or she would be able to provide more information than mere literal translations.

Ideally, this could be someone who receives some training in special education language and processes so that she can also explain the meaning behind the words themselves in greater detail to families. Additionally, as Ms. Klog suggests, materials themselves should be translated so that parents have equal access to them for review and to better prepare for meetings.

In this vein, Ms. Klog thinks that shifting the dynamics of the IEP meetings themselves to ensure a more conversational and less legalistic approach would improve the process for CLD families. Even native speakers have significant challenges navigating the highly technical IEP process. An added benefit of developing more authentic partnerships is that it would enable parents and school staff to jointly determine appropriate goals and to discuss the steps needed to help the student achieve the goals. Rather than coming together for the first time at the IEP meeting table, meeting with parents throughout the process—as Ms. Klog already does—could further open the channels of communication.

QUESTIONS FOR DISCUSSION/REFLECTION

- How important is the general education teacher's role in the IEP meetings for CLD students? How does a general education teacher's position shape his or her perspectives on the process?
- What are some ways teachers can rekindle their enthusiasm for teaching?
- How can teachers collect accurate information about new students?
- Short of hiring bilingual teachers, what are some ways schools can facilitate home-school communications?
- In an era when school district resources are stretched thin, what are some ways to provide general education teachers with support and training in identifying students who are CLD and might be eligible to receive special education services?
- In what ways could IEP meetings become less formal in discourse and more conversational? Who should take the lead in making this happen?
- Ms. Klog mentions "educationese" when describing the communication that takes place between the school and CLD families. What example(s) of "educationese" have you seen in your own practice?

NOTE

1. Child Study refers to a group of multidisciplinary professionals who consult with parents and teachers about available learning-related services.

ADDITIONAL RESOURCES

These articles, books, reports, and/or websites provide more information about the topics mentioned in this chapter.

Teacher Collaboration

Caskey, M. M., & Carpenter, J. (2014). Building teacher collaboration school-wide. *AMLE Magazine*. Retrieved from https://www.amle.org/BrowsebyTopic/WhatsNew/WNDet/TabId/270/ArtMID/888/ArticleID/446/Building-Teacher-Collaboration-School-wide.aspx

EdVestors. (2014). Making space: The value of teacher collaboration. Retrieved from https://www.edvestors.org/wp-content/uploads/2016/05/EdVestors-Making-Space-The-Value-of-Teacher-Collaboration-2014.pdf

Johnson, B. (2011). Making the most out of teacher collaboration. *Edutopia*. Retrieved from https://www.edutopia.org/blog/teacher-collaboration-strategies-ben-johnson

Ripley, S. (1997). *Collaboration between general and special education teachers*. ERIC EC Digest, ED4093171997. Retrieved from https://www.teachervision.com/teaching-strategies/collaboration-between-general-special-education-teachers

Teacher Dispositions

Aguilar, E. (2013). Six belief systems (extract from Teacher collaboration: When belief systems collide). *Edutopia*. Retrieved from https://backend.edutopia.org/sites/default/files/pdfs/blogs/edutopia-aguilar-ideologies-worksheet.pdf

Dottin, E. S. (2009). Professional judgment and dispositions in teacher education. *Teaching and Teacher Education, 25*(1), 83–88. https://doi-org.proxy.library.georgetown.edu/10.1016/j.tate.2008.06.005

Phelps, P. H. (2006). The dilemma of dispositions. *The Clearing House: A Journal of Strategies, Issues, and Ideas, 79*(4), 174–178. doi.org/10.3200/TCHS.79.4.174-178

University of Minnesota. (n.d.). Minnesota Educator Dispositions System strand 3: Collaboration and communication. Retrieved from https://sites.google.com/a/umn.edu/umn-dispositions-assessment-framework/dispositional-strands/rubrics/strand-3-rubric

Training General Education Teachers in Special Education

Council of Chief State School Officers (CCSSO). (n.d.) *Special education resources for general education teachers*. http://serge.ccsso.org/

European Agency for Development in Special Needs Education. (2010). *Teacher education for inclusion*. Retrieved from https://www.european-agency.org/sites/default/files/TE4I-Literature-Review.pdf

Singh, D. K. (2006). *Preparing general education teachers for inclusion*. ERIC ED 499-13. Retrieved from https://files.eric.ed.gov/fulltext/ED499013.pdf

Evaluating ESOL Students for Special Education Services

Minnesota Department of Education. (2005). *The ELL companion to reducing bias in special education.* Retrieved from http://www.asec.net/Archives/Manuals/ELL%20companion%20Manual%20020212[1].pdf

Smith, H. (2014). *Assessing ELLs for special education: 5 pitfalls to avoid.* Retrieved from https://www.scilearn.com/blog/assessing-ells-for-special-education-5-pitfalls-to-avoid

Chapter Three

The Special Education Teacher's Voice

"It's not that complicated."

In Individualized Education Program (IEP) meetings, the special education teacher plays a critical role, having closely followed a student's IEP, collected data to demonstrate progress toward the IEP's goals, and interacted with the student in a school context more frequently than most of the other school-based personnel at the table. Simply put, the special education teacher provides important information on student progress, effective instructional approaches, and areas to be addressed in the updated IEP (Dalien, 2014).

The special education teacher we interviewed, Ms. Matalino, is fluent in Spanish and has three years of special education teaching experience in a middle school for sixth through eighth graders. In her school, more than 10% of the students are dually identified and in need of both English for Speakers of Other Languages (ESOL) instruction and special education. There are two self-contained classes with a subgroup of these students, whom she calls "dualies."[1] One class is co-taught by a special education teacher and an ESOL teacher, and Ms. Matalino teaches the other. According to Ms. Matalino, most of the "dualies" with whom she works are Hispanic, although she recently had both an African and a Middle Eastern student in her classroom as well.

Ms. Matalino's school is in a district that is under the supervision of the U.S. Department of Justice (DOJ) for civil rights violations pertaining to the education of students who are English-language learners in special education, so she is directly impacted by DOJ interventions. In addition to reporting requirements beyond the standard IEP data collection, teachers working with dually identified students must participate in 15 hours of ESOL-related professional development annually for three years. Unfortunately, she believes that most of this professional development is really just about "checking off boxes" and that it is not an effective source of learning. As a result, she said, teachers are ill-prepared to deal with culturally and linguistically diverse (CLD) students.

PERSPECTIVES ON CULTURAL AND LINGUISTIC DIVERSITY

Ms. Matalino has had extensive dealings with parents from CLD backgrounds. The student population in the district where she works is comprised of nearly 70% CLD students, 40% economically disadvantaged students, and 16% ESOL students. She is bilingual in English and Spanish; although she is not of Hispanic origin, she is able to communicate directly with the Spanish-speaking parents of her students.

Parent Involvement

In Ms. Matalino's experience, there are differences in CLD parent involvement based on cultural and educational background. Overall, she believes that CLD parents are not necessarily helpful in obtaining appropriate special education services for their children. To start off with, she says, Hispanic parents are very respectful, but often have not had much formal schooling themselves. They may be limited in their availability and are frequently unable to attend meetings. In many cases, in her experience, their literacy skills are not sufficient to allow them to read the IEP, and they may just sign it and send it back to school. As a result, their input is minimal to nonexistent.

On the other hand, at the time that we interviewed her, Ms. Matalino was working with an African family who presented a different set of challenges. Unlike many Hispanic parents, she said, they had been able to read the IEP and seemed to understand everything. However, their involvement in the process has been largely damaging to their child's interest. They do not want special education services because they think their son is doing "fine" without them.

Unfortunately, the student is in eighth grade and, according to school assessments, has only second-grade reading skills and third-grade mathematics skills. In spite of those assessments, the parents do not want special education services because they do not want their son to bear what they consider a negative label. She reports that they have been very confrontational and that discussions have been counterproductive. In Ms. Matalino's view, this makes them much more like parents who speak English natively than those who do not.

As a result of these experiences, Ms. Matalino tends to hold a negative view of CLD families in general, although she says that she appreciates cultural diversity and continually attempts to undertake outreach and improve parent involvement in her classroom.

PERSPECTIVES ON THE IEP MEETING

Ms. Matalino's perspectives on IEP meetings with CLD parents focus on how to make the meetings a better experience for the families. In particular, she feels that the meetings could be more parent-friendly in terms of their logistics and that translation services could be improved overall.

Meeting Dynamics

At Ms. Matalino's school, a single administrator attends all IEP meetings involving "dualies," more than 100 students. Since one person handles all IEP meetings for "dualies," there are standard protocols in place. There is a very rigid seating protocol with the administrator at the head of the table sitting close to the exit in case she needs to leave unexpectedly. IEP meetings are scheduled for 30 minutes, although when an interpreter is needed, they expand the schedule to an hour. As a result, starting and ending on time are very important factors for a positive meeting.

Despite some elements of rigidity, each IEP meeting has its own tone and dynamic. Most teachers, Ms. Matalino believes, try to be positive and avoid confrontation, and overall communication during the IEP meetings is not a problem. Parents have already been through eligibility determinations and have had full explanations of their child's diagnosis and learning needs.

Most students, she adds, have a classification of learning disability (LD), so the IEP meetings are not complicated, and extensive justifications are not necessary. This is especially true when a teacher has conferred with a CLD parent in advance to address their concerns since parent comfort levels are important for a positive IEP meeting.

Sometimes, however, special education teachers do see CLD parents as acting defensively and spending a lot of energy making excuses for their children in order to minimize special educational needs and the school's recommendations for services. In such an environment, it is very important that special education and other school personnel explain their analysis and recommendations clearly, as using ill-defined or pejorative terms such as "deficit" only worsens the situation.

In these cases, Ms. Matalino attempts to explain that the school-based members of the IEP team are merely trying to "fill in the gaps," and that deficits are not the fault of the students. Nonetheless, CLD parents sometimes continue to resist the labels and interventions because they perceive services as stigmatizing. Such meetings can become antagonistic and unproductive, a concern shared by the principal (Chapter 1), the general education teacher (Chapter 2), the special education teacher (Chapter 3), the ESOL teacher (Chapter 4), the advocate (Chapter 5), the parent (Chapter 7), the translator (Chapter 8), and the guidance counselor (Chapter 12).

Translation and Interpretation

As noted above, the school provides interpretation for IEP meetings, and when an interpreter participates, meetings are scheduled for an hour rather than 30 minutes. Ms. Matalino remarked that because the interpreter extends the length of the meeting, staff hate having an interpreter present. While many of the required forms do exist in multiple languages, Ms. Matalino notes that IEP documents are provided only in English with no translation available. As such, the dynamics change when there is an interpreter who goes beyond direct translation to try to explain some of the processes behind the language.

An additional concern noted by Ms. Matalino is that there can be great variability among interpreters in terms of what they know and understand about special education processes and vocabulary. To mitigate this problem, teachers try to use simple language to explain the IEP goals and services. Nevertheless, due to the complexity of the IEP, comprehension is still difficult for many CLD parents.

Ms. Matalino herself sometimes serves as the translator due to her proficiency in Spanish, and in this role, she says she endeavors to ensure that there is no "us versus them" tenor to the meeting. Many others share this concern about the overall mood of IEP meetings with CLD families, including the principal (Chapter 1), the general education teacher (Chapter 2), the translator (Chapter 8), and the guidance counselor (Chapter 12).

SUGGESTIONS FOR IMPROVEMENT

It is unsurprising that Ms. Matalino's recommendations for improving IEP meetings with CLD families focus on making the meetings more welcoming to and accepting of parent involvement and input. In addition, she feels that both general and special education teachers need more experience in how to work with CLD families effectively.

Make IEP Meetings More Accessible

There are some small but important procedural elements that Ms. Matalino considers important to establishing a positive mood in IEP meetings. First, she thinks that flexible seating would relax everyone. It could also reduce the possibility of a contentious atmosphere by providing parents with freedom to sit where they are most comfortable. While this seems to be a small issue, it has come up in other conversations as well. Parents feel as though they are facing a phalanx of experts, which creates a sense of being outranked.

Next, it is important to avoid expressions from in-school personnel such as "we think," which can heighten a CLD parent's sense of being outnumbered. The focus should be on providing the parents with opportunities to express their opinions and provide input, rather than be expected to listen passively (Shafer, 2017). Ms. Matalino feels that discussing the student's strengths and areas of need together rather than following a scripted, formal presentation can go far toward achieving this.

Finally, rejecting any tendency to assign blame for a student's failings is critical, so that CLD parents are not put on the defensive and thus inclined to reject data and opinions from school staff. Because teachers are frustrated when parents become defensive, Ms. Matalino believes that making an effort to refrain from such tendencies would maintain a productive tone to the meeting.

Establish Trust

As others we interviewed have noted, trust between schools and CLD families is critical to successful IEP meetings. Establishing trust, however, often involves overcoming several barriers. In Ms. Matalino's experience, schools and teachers contact parents only when there is a problem, rather than developing a relationship beforehand. In addition, many CLD parents distrust schools due to experiences in their home countries. This creates a situation where more effective teacher outreach is necessary.

As a first step, Ms. Matalino emphasized that establishing trust with students themselves is crucial. Next, developing a relationship with parents is very important. This entails, at a minimum, touching base with parents before an IEP meeting to discuss the nature of the meeting, how parents should prepare, and who will be attending (e.g., Shafer, 2017). This will allow parents to ask questions in advance and go into the meeting more knowledgeable and confident that their child's teacher will be representing their interests.

Even better, teachers should encourage CLD students to bring their parents to any school event possible, so that parents can develop a level of comfort with the school environment overall prior to IEP meetings. Further, teachers should reach out throughout the school year to find out more information about students and their needs. Sometimes, a problem can be understood in a different light if a teacher knows more about a student's behaviors at home and his larger situation in life.

Train Teachers in CLD

Ms. Matalino mentions a lack of cultural competence as an obstacle to productive IEP meetings because IEP team members fail to grasp the very real cultural differences that influence parent participation and expectations for the school. The lack of these perspectives could explain some of the barriers that parents of her own students experience. In other words, understanding the situations in students' countries of origin and the educational cultures they have experienced would create a better understanding of why their parents interact with the school in the way that they do.

Ms. Matalino described how different CLD parent expectations can be when interacting with the schools. Because they do not automatically know the hidden "rules" for parent roles in their child's education or in their child's school, CLD parents might not appear to want to participate in the school community. For example, formal Parent-Teacher Associations (PTAs) or Parent Teacher Organizations (PTOs) do not exist in other countries. As such, CLD parents might not attend meetings or support these groups. However, many teachers and school officials, due to their lack of understanding of these cultural experiences and differences, do not realize this and simply assume that CLD parents are disinterested in their children's education.

Ms. Matalino emphasizes that there is a DOJ requirement at her school that teachers undertake professional development in cultural and linguistic diversity in education as a required remediation for equity in serving "dualies." She believes, however, that it is merely a token requirement, one that is not taken seriously by school staff and thus does not result in meaningful learning. While multicultural education courses are a requirement for initial licensure of some groups of teachers in some states, given the changing demographics of American schools, these courses are essential for all teachers (Maxwell, 2014; National Center for Educational Statistics, 2017b).

Moreover, even when such a requirement exists, it is extremely difficult to "teach" multicultural perspectives. Cultural competence emerges experientially through a process of extended contact and communication with individuals from other groups (Czop Assaf et al., 2010; Marquez Chisholm, 1994; Sleeter, 2016). Ms. Matalino suggests that a more meaningful approach would be a cultural inquiry process—regular teacher gatherings set up to explore perspectives, experiences, norms, and beliefs through dialogue across cultural and linguistic lines, and including the voices of school personnel from other cultural groups (Villegas & Lucas, 2002).

QUESTIONS FOR DISCUSSION/REFLECTION

- How important is the special education teacher's role in the IEP meetings for CLD students? How does a special education teacher's position shape his or her perspectives on the process?
- What are some ways to ensure that parents enjoy equal participation at the IEP table?
- What are some obstacles special education teachers face in undertaking outreach to parents? How might these be overcome?
- Do you believe that seating, time limits, and discourse patterns can have a significant impact on an IEP meeting? Why or why not?
- What can special education teachers do when they view the parents as an obstacle to their children's education?
- What experiences have you had in extended dialogue with members of cultural and linguistic groups that differ from your own? What have you learned from their perspectives?
- Do you think that federal intervention is effective in enacting reform for CLD families with children receiving special education services? Why or why not?

NOTE

1. In some quarters, this term is considered pejorative and/or dehumanizing.

ADDITIONAL RESOURCES

These articles, books, reports, and/or websites provide more information about the topics mentioned in this chapter.

Cultural Competence

Berman, P., Aburto, S., Nelson, B., Minicucci, C., & Burkart, G. (2000). *Going schoolwide: Comprehensive school reform inclusive of limited English proficient students.* Washington, DC: Office of Bilingual Education and Minority Language Affairs. Retrieved from http://www.ncbe.edu

Marquez Chisholm, I. (1994). Preparing teachers for multicultural classrooms. *Journal of Educational Issues of Language Minority Students, 14,* 43–68. Retrieved from http://www.edtechpolicy.org/ArchivedWebsites/chisholm.html

National Education Association. (2000). *Diversity toolkit.* Retrieved from http://www.nea.org/tools/diversity-toolkit.html

Villegas, A. M., & Lucas, T. (2002). *Educating culturally responsive teachers: A coherent approach.* Albany: State University of New York Press.

Vilson, J. (2015). *Empowering educators through cultural competence.* Retrieved from https://www.edutopia.org/blog/empowering-educators-through-cultural-competence-jose-vilson

IEP Meeting Dynamics

Bauserman, A. (2016). *The IEP meeting table: One perspective from two chairs.* Retrieved from https://www.pearsoned.com/iep-perspective-two-different-chairs/

Bollero, J. (2013). *8 steps to better IEP meetings: Play hearts, not poker.* Retrieved from http://www.wrightslaw.com/advoc/articles/iep.bollero.hearts.htm

Johnson, B. (2017). *How to make IEP meetings more effective.* Retrieved from https://www.edutopia.org/blog/how-make-iep-meetings-more-effective-ben-johnson

Shafer, L. (2017). *How to have a successful IEP meeting.* Retrieved from https://www.gse.harvard.edu/news/uk/17/09/how-have-successful-iep-meeting

Chapter Four

The ESOL Teacher's Voice

"Others just sit and watch . . . I get involved."

In an Individualized Education Program (IEP) meeting, the role of the English for Speakers of Other Languages (ESOL) teacher is to provide input on the student's performance and needs in the classroom, specifically in the area of cultural and language acquisition. Because ESOL teachers are familiar with the language acquisition process, they are able to describe and highlight particular needs related to language development.

ESOL teachers are also often able to note differences that others on the IEP team might otherwise attribute to general issues related to a student's status as a language learner rather than learning challenges that may reflect a need for specific special education services. ESOL teachers are also familiar with cultural challenges and issues related to families involved in the process, and they can sometimes draw on these perspectives to facilitate families' understanding of and involvement in the IEP process.

Ms. Hekima, the ESOL teacher we interviewed, has served culturally and linguistically diverse (CLD) students in U.S. public schools for more than 16 years. She has worked with students in grades 1 through 12, and she is bilingual (fluent in both Spanish and English). She holds an M.Ed. in Teaching English as a Second Language and is working on a doctorate in the same subject. She has also taught in teacher education programs at several local universities.

Ms. Hekima's first language is Spanish. Her family moved to the United States when she was in elementary school, and she completed middle and high school in a local district, where she later taught for several years. Her mother is also a bilingual teacher and serves the local immigrant community, including CLD students and families.

PERSPECTIVES ON CULTURAL AND LINGUISTIC DIVERSITY

Currently, Ms. Hekima works in a district with a very culturally and linguistically diverse population. District-wide, 20% of the students are English language learners, and they represent more than 100 countries. At her school, 34% of the students are Hispanic, 33% are white, 17% are African American, 13% are Asian, and 3% represent other groups or backgrounds. Besides working with middle school students during the day, she teaches in an ESOL program for parents in the evening and is a committed advocate for students and families.

In her role as an ESOL teacher, Ms. Hekima views herself as an equal rights advocate, particularly for CLD students with special education needs. As a result, she often attends IEP meetings serving as a teacher representative, but also as a cultural broker and as an advocate for students and families. She is committed to ensuring that the needs of CLD families are understood and that these families understand their rights and responsibilities within the educational system and the school community.

Cultural Mismatch

Due to her own experience as an immigrant, Ms. Hekima understands firsthand many of the cultural and linguistic challenges faced by families who are new to the United States, particularly those with Spanish-speaking origins. As a teacher in a U.S. district, she sees the mismatch of cultural expectations between families whose experience leads them to believe that school personnel are the experts and American schools that expect parents to be active in communicating with teachers and school personnel.

The mismatch is exacerbated when parents lack formal education and feel inhibited by their limited English-language skills. Ms. Hekima is active in working with these parents, staying after school into the evenings to work on parent education efforts aimed at teaching not only how to speak English but also how to navigate the school system. She stated that some parents are afraid of involvement with the school system because they do not understand the system, do not speak or read English well enough to understand the documents that their children bring home, and/or do not having advanced education.

Cultural Advocacy

Ms. Hekima's advocacy for CLD families in the IEP process emerged as she saw some of the misunderstandings her district's special education personnel had regarding language issues, the status of dual enrollment, and overrepresentation of CLD students in some categories of disability. Because misunderstandings on both the side of the parents and the side of school officials abound, she views her role of advocate as an important one, particularly in ensuring equal access to special education services. As a department chair, she frequently attends special education meetings and perpetually attempts to build bridges between schools and parents.

Ms. Hekima became involved in advocating for CLD students in need of special education services early in her career as an ESOL teacher. One year, she had a student whose family had moved to the United States because their local special education services were inadequate for the needs of their child. Unlike many of the families she works with, these parents had a strong sense of their child's needs, came with documentation from local evaluations (although those were in Spanish, from their home country), and a determination to secure services so that their child did not fall behind in school. When Ms. Hekima initiated a referral process based on the documentation she had received from his parents, the special education office replied that they should wait at least one year before acting because the student was new to the country.

Since then, Ms. Hekima has seen numerous inequities in the area of special education for CLD students and families, which have led her to believe that there is no such thing as equitable education. In her view, if a student is white, wealthy, and educated, his family receives a strong IEP. For CLD families, this is seldom the case. Another problem is that CLD families tend to trust the system, but the system is not doing what it should for them.

She compared two cases, a Hispanic student with Down syndrome and a white student who shared the same diagnosis. Both students had a problem with wandering. School officials decided that the Hispanic wanderer needed to be sent to a special school, while the white student remained at his base school. While Ms. Hekima was not privy to the reasons underlying this decision, she is convinced that language issues and parent advocacy contributed to the divergent outcomes for these two students.

Generally, Ms. Hekima believes that equity is lacking because of misunderstandings and politics rather than because of malice. First, on a technical level, there is no distinct "line" between language acquisition and processing and special education. Further, staff sometimes neglect to include perspectives from ESOL teachers that could illuminate which issues are typical in second-language acquisition and which are likely related to additional factors or learning differences.

In addition, when obtaining a positive eligibility determination, there is an equal-access problem. CLD students are not always tested when needed because the county fears overidentification of some demographic groups. Ms. Hekima has even heard from special education specialists the erroneous but definitively delivered statement that, due to a language barrier, CLD students are not eligible for any special education services.

PERSPECTIVES ON THE IEP MEETING

Ms. Hekima has sat in numerous IEP meetings, and it is there that she most frequently gets involved when she sees bias or misconceptions. While ESOL teachers are not expected to play a significant role in many cases—and sometimes are not even included in meetings—when present, she does her best to mediate across the cultural divides that can emerge during the meetings. She shared numerous recurrent dynamics and phenomena that typify such meetings.

Pre-Meeting Communication

Communication is fraught with the potential for misunderstandings, and CLD parents are often confused about the purposes, processes, meanings, and implications of meetings. First, parents are often confused about why they have been called into the school for a meeting. There can also be misconceptions about the nature of the meeting. One parent, for example, arrived at the meeting thinking that all students had this kind of educational review and planning session.

Next, even when they do understand that their child has been identified for some kind of educational review because he needs services, CLD parents do not understand all of the documents involved in the special education correspondence and eligibility determination, or even the IEP document itself. While there is usually translation for meetings, there is no requirement that the documents be translated, so parents often come to meetings overwhelmed and in the dark.

Finally, even when they do have a sense of the documents and their purposes, CLD parents are often confused as to the meaning of the language itself, the classification, the nature of services and delivery proposed, and what the implications are for their child. Translators translate the language, but the language is complex, nuanced, and often inaccessible to anyone not versed in education. Translation is a frequently mentioned issue, as evident in discussions with the principal (Chapter 1), the general education teacher (Chapter 2), the translator (Chapter 8), and the guidance counselor (Chapter 12).

Conflicting Agendas

In Ms. Hekima's experience, during an IEP meeting with CLD families, "There are a lot of people tugging at the agenda," including the district special education coordinator, the school psychologist, the special education department chair, and sometimes specialists, besides the general education and ESOL teachers. Frequently, these participants have discussion and debate among themselves prior to the start of the meeting, and others—parents, and general education and ESOL teachers—"just sit and watch." During this organizational time, there is no translation because the meeting has not yet officially begun, so parents are unsure from the outset about the procedures that will follow.

Once the meeting begins, the meeting leader may ask for reports from the physical and/or occupational therapist, speech/language pathologists, or other specialists involved in the IEP. The translators cover the report contents as they proceed. However, the language and content, even in translation, are not necessarily clear and accessible to those not versed in the field. Some parents do ask questions, but many are so overwhelmed that they would rather keep quiet. In many instances, this dynamic persists throughout the entire meeting.

When parents are quiet and seem overwhelmed, the parent liaison and ESOL teacher may take on the role of advocate, asking for explanations and clarifications and providing further input for parents. They may suggest specific interventions based on their understanding of the situation. Doing so, however, can lead to an "us versus them" dynamic, with the special education team discounting the input on language and culture as irrelevant or categorizing the student's needs as related to language acquisition rather than processing or other learning challenges. The principal (Chapter 1), the general education teacher (Chapter 2), the special education teacher (Chapter 3), the advocate (Chapter 5), the parent (Chapter 7), the translator (Chapter 8), the school psychologist (Chapter 9), the specialist (Chapter 10), and the guidance counselor (Chapter 12) share these concerns.

The Role of the ESOL Teacher

Ms. Hekima has had difficulty establishing that ESOL teachers are important participants in the IEP process and meetings. While ESOL teachers are supposed to provide input for the statement on the Present Level of Performance (PLOP) page, for example, their contributions are often not included. In some cases, ESOL teachers themselves are excluded from meetings, meaning that there can be no input on the process of language acquisition, instructional strategies, or progress in learning English, reading, and writing.

ESOL teachers often need to bring evidence that a child lacks understanding and skills in his first language as well as in English. Even then, there is a misperception that this is the result of deficient instruction and that the student needs to learn English prior to receiving services. Overall, Ms. Hekima said, the relationship between ESOL and the other school-based personnel in IEP meetings is a fraught one, and she often feels that she is not taken seriously. Beyond meetings, she feels that schoolwide, ESOL teachers are not respected as professionals and that, in general, they are treated like second-class citizens within the school community.

SUGGESTIONS FOR IMPROVEMENT

In light of her experiences, Ms. Hekima has numerous suggestions for improvements in the areas of training, communication, and meeting dynamics. In her view, training and education for parents, teachers, and translators would improve the process and communication among stakeholders, and better home-school communications would enhance mutual understanding and improve the educational effectiveness for students. Developing strategies for promoting respect and equality among members of the IEP would also improve the dynamics of meetings as well as educational results.

Check the Balance of Power

Based on Ms. Hekima's discussion, a significant area for improvement lies in the IEP meeting dynamics, which are currently characterized by a significant power imbalance. Special education teachers and staff have predetermined views about a student's diagnosis, needs, and appropriate educational approaches, and they discuss these without much regard for parent input. Parents, who have received little comprehensible input in advance of the meeting, face the daunting task of following technical discussions and thus feel intimidated. Parents simply do not know how to process so much information in an hour or two. School officials speak *to* parents but not *with* parents. As a result, IEP meetings occur, but there is no real conversation.

According to Ms. Hekima, altering the pace of meetings, explaining the nature of a student's challenges, providing concrete examples of points being made, and discussing possible approaches are strategies that have worked in the past. School staff could also be active in engaging parents by offering options and asking them for their input and opinion. Put simply, CLD parents need to understand the process and approaches in order to make sense of them. They know their children and want what is best, linguistically, technically, educationally, and culturally, but they are all too often overwhelmed.

On a practical level, translation should begin once parents arrive, so that once the formal meeting begins, they do not feel excluded from the conversation. Principals or other attending administrators should make an extra effort to ensure that everyone is at ease and in agreement about the agenda, the purposes of the meeting, and the procedures involved in the IEP process. Developing training for parents, teachers, and translators can contribute to resolution of some of these issues.

Help Teachers Develop Cultural Competence

In Ms. Hekima's view, teacher education efforts should focus on the area of cultural competence. Due to cultural differences, misunderstandings can quickly emerge and undermine home-school relationships that would other-wise function to support a student's education. This is consistent with find-ings that teachers are not adequately prepared to work with students from CLD backgrounds (Park & Thomas, 2012). The misunderstandings run both ways—hence the need for parent education, to understand the culture of U.S. schools. Remediating with some education for teachers working with CLD students would greatly improve the IEP experience. It would also help those teachers generally in communicating with all parents, not merely CLD par-ents or parents involved with an IEP.

Cultural differences can be major or minor. In some cultures, for exam-ple, eye contact is considered a form of disrespect. In American culture, however, teachers may interpret lack of eye contact as disinterest, disrespect, or even dishonesty. On a larger level, in many other cultures, teachers are revered as a source of education and wisdom—a great contrast to the view in American culture, where teaching remains a relatively low-status profession. Due to their reverence for teachers, many CLD parents would never consider contacting a teacher with questions or suggestions regarding instructional approaches. In their view, teachers are the experts, and such questions would constitute a significant breach of cultural norms.

A barrier to this type of professional development, however, is the rigid-ity of some teachers. Many do want training in the specific cultural norms, history, and expectations of the CLD students in their classroom population. Some teachers, however, do not want this and consider their ways to be the "right" ones to which students and parents should conform. More significant-ly, many enjoy working with populations that do not interfere and pose questions. Some teachers do not live up to the trust placed in them by CLD parents, and as a result, students may not receive the same level of attention and services as those whose parents are monitoring instructional interven-tions more closely.

Another area that is rife with misunderstandings is eligibility for special education for CLD students. Ms. Hekima has often heard from special educa-tion colleagues that CLD students are not eligible for services or evaluation due to language barriers or not having lived in the district for a certain period of time. This is untrue and has in fact been an area investigated at the federal level in districts across the United States to ensure equality of access as well as to avoid overclassification (U.S. Department of Education, 2018). Teach-ers—special education, general education, and ESOL teachers alike—need training for clarity on this topic.

Besides training in eligibility and classification, teachers need cross-disci-plinary training so that general and special education teachers can understand language acquisition. ESOL and general education teachers must be educated about various types of disabilities and their manifestations, such as process-ing deficits, sensory issues, and social challenges. In this way, teachers can more effectively collaborate based on their understanding of students' needs to determine effective instructional approaches.

Help Parents Understand Special Education

In addition to training for teachers, educating CLD parents of special education students about the process itself is critical. Parents need to know their rights and responsibilities, and understand the roles of special education, general education, and ESOL teachers and their interactions with their child. As noted, in many cultures, parents tend to view schools as centers of authority and expertise, resulting in a situation where parents trust the system, but the system may not be doing what is best for their children, partially due to a lack of parental input.

One way to create a more informed and active parent population might be a special "IEP 101" seminar, which could start with a workshop where parents learn about identifying students for services, making a diagnosis, and the testing process. Subsequent workshops could target understanding the development of IEPs or possible accommodations. Ensuring that parents realize that their contributions to developing educational and social goals for their children are both appropriate and necessary will help parents feel more empowered in discussions and meetings. Finally, informing parents about the role of data and reporting will provide them with the opportunity for a more active role in monitoring their children's educational progress.

While Ms. Hekima's district has a parent education center, the problem, she says, is logistical. Parents who live at a distance do not make frequent use of the center's resources due to transportation challenges and the fact that they do not have relationships at such a center. Far better, she thinks, would be to offer parent workshops at their children's schools. Because some parents, who may lack formal education themselves, may fear involvement in education, the role of outreach by a parent liaison with linguistic and cultural connections to the parent community is critical in this process.

Help Translators Understand Special Education

First, to more adequately explain the meeting procedures, translators need training on disabilities, IEP goals and measures, and special education services in general. Next, prior to meetings, they also should also be briefed by school personnel on a particular IEP situation. As frequently noted, technical translation does not suffice because the language and process is so complex that even native speakers can find it daunting. In addition, while the IEP document does not have to be translated, some attempt to communicate with parents in their first language prior to the meeting would provide them time to process the extraordinarily heavy informational load that emerges during meetings.

An additional barrier is translation for less common languages. In Ms. Hekima's county there are more than 100 languages spoken. Of these, however, interpreters are only available for the eight most commonly spoken languages. While this is clearly a resource issue, it is one that is fairly easy to remediate with small additional investment. Among the local populations, there is likely a fluent speaker of English who could participate in special education training for teachers and translators and serve to assist families, even if not providing formal translation.

Improve Communication

To strengthen the impact of this training, all stakeholders in the IEP process should increase their communication with one another. With training, parents should feel more empowered to ask questions, to request changes in meeting times, and to discuss the needs of their child. Meeting leaders need to encourage this input to ensure a fuller picture of a student's needs, progress, and areas of challenge.

On the part of the schools, greater outreach could improve these linkages as well. In some cases, for example, parents receive the documents by mail and are informed of a meeting time, rather than presented with options for discussion or input on mutually agreeable meeting times. If they have to work or face a loss of pay for taking time off, they may not attend the meeting and are unlikely to understand its importance. Schools in turn may interpret this nonattendance as a lack of interest. In addition, schools could develop a policy of following up on document mailings with contact by a bilingual parent liaison who can help the parents develop questions for teachers and others involved in the IEP. The parent liaison could also help to negotiate a time conducive to full participation by family members.

In order to develop relationships that will result in more participatory IEP meetings, teachers and specialists can also undertake greater outreach, ensuring that translators are available for conferences and offering alternative times and means of conferencing for working parents. Often parents who are knowledgeable about the special education process contact teachers and specialists or proactively request weekly updates. CLD parents may not consider this an appropriate request, or it may be something they would never think of asking.

The misunderstandings described by Ms. Hekima do not seem to be driven by antipathy, but ensue from a lack of knowledge and communication. Actively considering ways to improve understanding of roles, cultures, and interventions will improve the experience for all and will likely result in better outcomes for families and students. This in turn will contribute to helping students achieve their potential and successfully transition to the larger world and society.

QUESTIONS FOR DISCUSSION/REFLECTION

- How important is the ESOL teacher's role in the IEP meetings for CLD students? How does an ESOL teacher's position shape his or her perspectives on the process?
- How can ESOL and special education teachers more effectively work together to benefit students? How can building administrators facilitate this? District-level administrators?
- Do you think that the marginalization of ESOL teachers is a general problem? Why or why not?
- Can an ESOL teacher who does not have Ms. Hekima's background be successful with CLD students who receive special education services? Why or why not?
- If translation of meetings is the only legal requirement, what are some ways that parents can more readily access background information regarding their child's IEP?
- Besides the recommendations listed here for improving home-school communications, what other possibilities exist?
- To what extent do you believe that Ms. Hekima's recommendations are realistic?

ADDITIONAL RESOURCES

These articles, books, reports, and/or websites provide more information about the topics mentioned in this chapter.

Bridging the Home-School Divide

Berman, P., Aburto, S., Nelson, B., Minicucci, C., & Burkart, G. (2000). *Going schoolwide: Comprehensive school reform inclusive of limited English proficient students.* Washington, DC: Office of Bilingual Education and Minority Language Affairs. Retrieved from http://www.ncela.ed.gov/files/rcd/BE020926/Going_Schoolwide_Comprehensive.pdf

Howland, A., Anderson, J. A., Smiley, A. D., & Abbott, D. J. (2006). School liaisons: Bridging the gap between home and school. *School Community Journal, 16*(2), 47–68.

Quinton, S. (2013). Good teachers embrace their students' cultural backgrounds. *The Atlantic.* Retrieved from https://www.theatlantic.com/education/archive/2013/11/good-teachers-embrace-their-students-cultural-backgrounds/281337/

Cultural Differences in Schools

Alrubail, R. (2016). Being mindful of cultural differences. *Edutopia.* Retrieved from https://www.edutopia.org/discussion/being-mindful-cultural-differences

Banks, J. (2001). Multicultural education programs evaluation checklist. In J. Banks (Ed.), *Cultural diversity and education* (4th ed.) (pp. 336–344). Boston: Allyn & Bacon.

Irvine, J. J. (2009). Relevant: Beyond the basics. *Teaching Tolerance, 36.* Retrieved from https://www.tolerance.org/magazine/fall-2009/relevant-beyond-the-basics

ESOL and Special Education

Ensmann, A. (2003). Identifying special education needs in ESOL students: Is it a language issue or a disability? Fairfax Public Schools. Retrieved from https://gse.gmu.edu/assets/docs/lmtip/vol2/A.Ensmann.doc

Mathews, K. (2016). ESOL and special education collaboration: A teacher's perspective. *Color in Colorado.* Retrieved from http://www.colorincolorado.org/article/esol-and-special-education-collaboration

Piazza, S. V., Rao, S., & Protacio, M. S. (2015). Converging recommendations for culturally responsive literacy practices: Students with learning disabilities, English language learners, and socioculturally diverse learners. *International Journal of Multicultural Education, 17*(3), 1–20.

Chapter Five

The Advocate's Voice

"There should be no hidden agendas—
this is someone's life."

An Individualized Education Program (IEP) meeting does not require the presence of a third-party educational advocate.[1] When part of the IEP team, the advocate is there to serve as the family's representative and to argue for the needs of the student. In most cases, the presence of an advocate is a signal that the family of the student feels that a third party will be helpful in securing the services needed. As Ms. Amamihe, the advocate we interviewed, put it, "When they [the school personnel] see me, they know they are failing."

Ms. Amamihe is the mother of two children with special needs. She describes herself as outspoken by nature, adding, "I say what I think!" For example, while she prefers that an IEP meeting be congenial, she is quick to tell team members that "we're not friends," lest they misconstrue her pleasantness for lack of determination.

In addition to working on behalf of her own children for nearly 20 years, Ms. Amamihe is a former general education teacher of English at the secondary level. Although there are no federal or state guidelines addressing the credentialing requirements for an individual to serve as an advocate, Ms. Amamihe has attended more than 30 inservices on topics such as applied behavior analysis (ABA), functional behavior assessments (FBAs), and special education law.

Observing that "business is booming," Ms. Amamihe attributes her success to her ability to "think outside the box" and her willingness to "drive a wedge [between families and school personnel] to get the student a better life." In other words, Ms. Amamihe believes that "being polite doesn't necessarily get you anywhere."

PERSPECTIVES ON CULTURAL AND LINGUISTIC DIVERSITY

Ms. Amamihe's views on cultural and linguistic diversity in general stem from her experiences working one-on-one with parents. The nature of her role as advocate often results in her getting to know the family on a deeply personal level. Ms. Amamihe feels that the intimacy that comes with providing advice to parents who are experiencing a myriad of emotions and who are in a difficult situation leads her to view the team's interactions through their eyes.

The Impact of Emotions

In addition to feeling wary of the motives of school-based personnel, Ms. Amamihe notes that most culturally and linguistically diverse (CLD) parents with whom she works are also angry. They often feel as though they deserve an apology from the school, and when none is forthcoming, bitter feelings arise. Further, parents sometimes go beyond hoping for an apology and convince themselves that the school personnel are lying to or keeping secrets from them.

Ms. Amamihe suggests that there would be more trust if schools were more honest with CLD families from the beginning. Instead, she has noticed that teachers try to convince parents that they (the teachers) like the student on a personal level, and thus really do have the child's best interests in mind. Ms. Amamihe's view is that a teacher's personal feelings should have nothing do with a child's education, saying "Love is not a part of the special education teacher's job description."

One final emotional aspect noted by Ms. Amamihe is that school personnel feel overwhelmed by and under-resourced to meet the needs of students they think of as "challenging," and that school personnel *always* consider CLD students to be "challenging." In Ms. Amamihe's opinion, the view that CLD students are "hard to handle" is often due to a lack of consistency in terms of teachers' skills with regard to special education pedagogy, cultural competence, and accurate data collection.

PERSPECTIVES ON THE IEP MEETING

In her experience, Ms. Amamihe has observed that, if a student's parents speak a language other than English or if they have a disability themselves, their treatment by the schools is "far worse." She frequently hears CLD parents report that they do not receive newsletters from the classroom or announcements from the school or that school personnel attempt to exert power by setting arbitrary meeting dates and times and by being inflexible in terms of rescheduling. This sets off a vicious cycle. Being excluded or disregarded leads to feelings of mistrust and, in turn, feelings of mistrust negatively affect the development and maintenance of respect between CLD families and school personnel, not to mention that mistrust also feeds into already present feelings of anger and confusion.

Differential Treatment

When asked about her experiences working on IEP teams on behalf of families who are culturally and linguistically diverse, Ms. Amamihe puts it bluntly: "White, English-speaking parents get a different IEP." For example, she has witnessed interpreters being instructed by school personnel to share "only the basics" of the IEP with families in a deliberate attempt to keep the parents vulnerable to being uninformed.

Another common occurrence for families who are culturally and linguistically diverse is what Ms. Amamihe calls "the meeting before the meeting" (as mentioned by the parent in Chapter 7) in which school personnel meet to discuss the IEP without the family present. In Ms. Amamihe's opinion, this not only violates procedural safeguards, it also leads families to feel that schools keep secrets, which undermines equality and fosters feelings of mistrust.

Defensiveness

If Ms. Amamihe sees herself as a divisive element in IEP meetings, it should come as no surprise that she feels that these can often be "recipes for disaster." She explains this by noting that—by the time she is present at an IEP meeting—school personnel and families are often overwhelmed and thus are acting on the defensive. There are many reasons for this defensiveness.

For one, from the school's perspective, the stakes are high. Ms. Amamihe's presence is a very visible reminder that parents are unhappy and thus could be contemplating legal action, which makes administrators understandably nervous and "on edge." As a result, administrators tell teachers to "keep their mouths shut" so as to avoid any concern regarding the school's liability.

The stakes are also high from the family's perspective. For CLD parents, IEP meetings are often occasions to feel both anger and guilt—anger at the sense of being "cheated" by the lack of services offered, and guilt due to a belief that they have somehow failed their child. In addition, parents are often still mourning the fact that their child is not "normal" and, as a consequence, are also ashamed of the situation.

In Ms. Amamihe's experience, these heightened emotions can result in parents being "unreasonable" and becoming "barriers" to the process by refusing to accept any compromise offered by school personnel. Thus, if school personnel are hesitant to share with parents what they consider to be "bad" news (i.e., "Your child is not progressing") and parents are reluctant to work with school personnel, the IEP meeting becomes a constant power struggle—a "disaster" for all involved.

Another emotion that Ms. Amamihe has often seen in IEP meetings for CLD students is pity. The school personnel sometimes express that they feel sorry for the situation, the parents, and the student. Ms. Amamihe believes that schools should spend less time communicating their sympathy and more time demonstrating that they understand the situation, the parents, and the student. One way in which this lack of understanding is conveyed is when school personnel use technical or confusing language and acronyms. As Ms. Amamihe puts it, "Schools need to know who they are talking to."

The Role of the Advocate

In much the same vein, Ms. Amamihe believes that advocates should also be aware of who they are and their role in the process. She has witnessed many colleagues electing to remain relatively silent during an IEP meeting in order to maintain a positive relationship with the local educational agency (LEA). For example, advocates will sometimes refrain from "pushing back" on something said by the school because they know they will be likely to work with the school again on behalf of another client.

The need to avoid contention, ensure understanding, and minimize an "us versus them" dynamic is an issue discussed by many others: the principal (Chapter 1), the general education teacher (Chapter 2), the special education teacher (Chapter 3), the ESOL teacher (Chapter 4), the parent (Chapter 7), the translator (Chapter 8), and the guidance counselor (Chapter 12). Ms. Amamihe believes that the best meetings are ones that are open and characterized by a "meet in the middle" approach.

However, Ms. Amamihe also feels that, in most cases, "An IEP meeting *should* be negative." Given that IEPs are—by their very nature—concerned with deficits in a student's performance and/or achievement rather than their successes, Ms. Amamihe firmly believes that all IEP team members should be committed to being honest about what is (and is not) working for a student.

SUGGESTIONS FOR IMPROVEMENT

Ms. Amamihe's suggestions for improvement for IEP meetings stem primarily from the interpersonal relationships and perceptions of those who sit at the table. These include helping school-based personnel learn to deliver information that might be difficult for parents to hear in an effective way, and having the principal present at all meetings.

Have the Courage of Convictions

Ms. Amamihe believes that the only way for an IEP meeting to avoid being a "disaster" is for everyone involved to be as transparent as possible. IEP meetings can be fraught with emotion. There can be feelings of mistrust, frustration, and uncertainty among all team members. When an advocate is present, school personnel can feel that the stakes are especially high, making it difficult for them to say what needs to be said.

The fear that being honest and saying "Your child is not successful" outright will hurt feelings and/or cause additional tension prevents teachers from being more forthcoming. In addition, the fear that delivering "bad" news to a family might result in losing one's position in the school is also a deterrent to a teacher's being open and honest about a student's classroom performance. As a result, Ms. Amamihe suggests that schools should adopt a "whistleblower" type of policy in which teachers need not fear reprisals from the administration if they share data that is considered negative or evidence of a lack of progress.

Develop a Better "Deskside Manner"

Similarly, Ms. Amamihe feels that teachers and other school personnel also need training in how to deliver "bad" news as impartially as possible. For example, the adoption of what Fleischman and Imaz-Marial (2015) call a "deskside framework" or "an educator's ability to communicate and interact with students in a manner that establishes stability . . . through the creation of trust, comfort and confidence in an ongoing professional relationship with students" (pp. 83–84) would prove beneficial. While originally discussed with university students in mind, the focus of the "deskside framework" on showing respect, listening critically, the "Four Bs" (being thorough, being clear, being honest, and being firm), and following up could be a helpful approach in IEP meetings with CLD families and prevent these from devolving into being nonproductive.

Require the Presence of the Principal

By law, either a principal or a principal's designee must attend an IEP meeting. In Ms. Amamihe's view, when the latter is present, it sends a bad message to families. In essence, it communicates that the principal has better things to do or that the student and her/his family do not merit the principal's time.

In some cultures, the absence of an established authority figure to be "in charge" would be puzzling or insulting. In other words, when the principal is not there at the meeting, the already heightened sense of tension and/or anxiety can be even more elevated. As a result, Ms. Amamihe suggests that principals attend as many IEP meetings as they can, especially those with CLD families, so that misunderstandings can be avoided and trust can be built and maintained.

QUESTIONS FOR DISCUSSION/REFLECTION

- How important is the advocate's role in the IEP meetings for CLD students? How does an advocate's position shape his or her perspectives on the process?
- What hidden or competing agendas might be at work in IEP meetings with CLD families?
- What do you think Ms. Amamihe means by the statement that "An IEP meeting *should* be negative"? To what extent do you agree or disagree?
- What resources have you found helpful when you have had to deliver "bad" news?
- "Bedside manner" is a concept more common in medicine than in education. How would you define "bedside manner" and its role in special education and/or working with CLD families?
- What are your own thoughts on Ms. Amamihe's statement, "Love is not a part of the special education teacher's job description"? Do you agree or disagree? Why?
- Ms. Amamihe argues that "Schools need to know who they are talking to." How might school personnel go about getting to know CLD families in a meaningful way?

NOTE

1. Advocate and consultant are often used interchangeably. While there are many overlaps in terms of their duties, school personnel often report that they prefer to work with the latter because they are seen as less confrontational.

ADDITIONAL RESOURCES

These articles, books, reports, and/or websites provide more information about the topics mentioned in this chapter.

Educational Advocacy

Center for Special Education Advocacy: http://www.advocacyinstitute.org

Hoover, J. J., & deBettencourt, L. U. (2017). Educating culturally and linguistically diverse exceptional learners: The need for continued advocacy. *Exceptionality, 26*, 176–189. https://10.1080/09362835.2017.1299530

National Special Education Advocacy Institute: https://www.nseai.org

Collaboration

Norris, K. E. L., & Collier, S. (2018). *Social justice and parent partnerships in multicultural education contexts.* Hershey, PA: IGI Global.

Olivos, E. M., Gallagher, R. J., & Aguilar, J. (2010). Fostering collaboration with culturally and linguistically diverse families of children with moderate to severe disabilities. *Journal of Educational and Psychological Consultation, 20,* 28–40. https://10.1080/10474410903535372

Rossetti, Z., Sauer, J. S., & Bui, O. (2017). Developing collaborative partnerships with culturally and linguistically diverse families. *Teaching Exceptional Children, 49,* 328–338.

Verdon, S., Wong, S., & McLeod, S. (2015). Shared knowledge and mutual respect: Enhancing culturally competent practice through collaboration with families and communities. *Child Language Teaching and Therapy, 32,* 205–221. Retrieved from http://journals.sagepub.com/doi/10.1177/0265659015620254

Professional Development for Advocates

Local Educational Agency (LEA) Universe Survey Data:https://nces.ed.gov/ccd/pubagency.asp

von Ravensburg, H., & Blakely, A. (2015). When to use functional behavioral assessment? A state-by-state analysis of the law. Positive Intervention and Behavioral Supports Online, October. Retrieved from https://www.pbis.org/Common/Cms/files/pbisresources/EvalBrief_Oct2015.pdf

Wrightslaw: http://www.wrightslaw.com

Chapter Six

The Disability Rights Attorney's Voice

"It's emotionally and legally complex."

As is the case with an advocate, an Individualized Education Program (IEP) meeting does not require the presence of a disability rights attorney. When one is present as part of the IEP team, the disability rights attorney is there on behalf of the family to advocate for the student's civil rights under the Individuals with Disabilities Education Act (IDEA) and Section 504 of the Rehabilitation Act for students with disabilities. Typically, the presence of a disability rights attorney is a signal that the family of the student has concerns about the special education process that might necessitate litigation.

The disability rights attorney we interviewed, Ms. Ologbon, was first drawn to special education law through her experience as the mother of three children with special needs. As an attorney with 24 years of experience in the areas of special education and disability rights, she has represented hundreds of clients in school disciplinary hearings and counseled them regarding disability rights and benefits. In addition, she has also served as a court-appointed special advocate for abused and neglected children and as a guardian ad litem for abused children, investigating custody solutions that are in the best interests of such children. She sums up her responsibilities this way: "I try to see my clients like I see my own children."

PERSPECTIVES ON CULTURAL AND LINGUISTIC DIVERSITY

Ms. Ologbon's experience is that working with culturally and linguistically diverse (CLD) families can be "very, very hard." They require a nuanced

49

understanding of many factors, which sometimes results in disproportionality in every respect.

Language Barriers

As mentioned by many others—the principal (Chapter 1), the general education teacher (Chapter 2), the ESOL teacher (Chapter 4), the translator (Chapter 8), and the guidance counselor (Chapter 12)—perhaps the biggest challenge to successful communication is the language barrier. Although translators are sometimes present in schools, simultaneous translation is difficult. This is even more challenging if the family is unable to read or write in their native language.

Language barriers serve to undermine the trust necessary for an effective working relationship, an issue mentioned by all but the transition specialist (Chapter 11). Ms. Ologbon refers to trust as a "huge" issue. Although it is easy to lose (for reasons previously discussed), it is tough to build or regain. Another factor related to ineffective communication is the school's tendency to focus on the negative. Families often hear about so many problems that they find themselves wondering if their child does anything right. In addition, schools can be hesitant to admit when a mistake has been made for fear of making things worse for the district.

Cultural Differences

There are differences in culture to contend with as well. These differences manifest themselves in the varying expectations and biases regarding education held by both school personnel and families. For example, as others have noted, CLD families tend to trust the school and its personnel, perhaps to a greater degree than is warranted. They feel that the teachers and administrators are professionals and, as such, can be counted on to "do the right thing" when it comes to their children.

As a result, CLD parents might not attend conferences or respond to notes home because they are confident that the teachers can (and will) handle any issue that arises. However, in the United States, teachers often hold the assumption that "good" parents are involved parents. By showing up for conferences and responding to notes, parents are demonstrating that they are invested and interested in their child's education. Parents who do not do these things are thought of as "bad" because their lack of participation suggests an uncaring or apathetic attitude.

When talking about her pro bono work with students who are culturally and linguistically diverse, Ms. Ologbon remarks that "everything is clear, but nothing is clear." As she straddles the line between due process and litigation, Ms. Ologbon is clear that her primary role as an advocate is to do what is best for the student. What is often unclear is what families want or think they need for their child. For example, parents might know what options are available to their child, or they might insist on one particular option such as a placement in a private school. As such, Ms. Ologbon only works with CLD families whose expectations are grounded in the reality of what the system can offer.

These concerns lead Ms. Ologbon to point out that working with a CLD family is in many respects an exercise in maintaining balance between costs and benefits for all involved. As a result, she remarks, "I don't get jaded, but I do get tired." Ms. Ologbon's optimism stems from the fact that she does see many positives in the special education process, even though the Individuals with Disabilities Education Act (IDEA) is not fully funded.

PERSPECTIVES ON THE IEP MEETING

Because Ms. Ologbon approaches every IEP meeting as though it will be entered as evidence in a legal proceeding, she is very methodical in her approach. When parents initially contact her, she reads the child's current IEP in its entirety. Then, she talks to the family and—assuming that the parents are open to options besides due process—shares a list of questions (based on the child's IEP) that parents should in turn share with the school. In doing this, Ms. Ologbon feels that she has more control over the conversation, everyone comes prepared, and the IEP meeting is less defensive.

Knowledge of Special Education Law

These preparations highlight Ms. Ologbon's view that IEP meetings involving CLD families are different from the ones she attends for Caucasian children. As she bluntly states, "You are more inclined to get what you want if you are White." Based on her experience, Ms. Ologbon feels that it is often the case that schools refuse or defer services to children from CLD families because the families are not aware of the rights and responsibilities associated with due process. But, interestingly, it is not only the families who are unaware.

Regarding ways to improve the effectiveness of IEP meetings with CLD families, Ms. Ologbon is quick to note that principals and teachers are often ignorant of the provisos of special education law and the resources the law can provide. Further exacerbating the issue, school personnel are often "burned out" and have little cultural understanding. A telling example of the latter is the time when Ms. Ologbon attended an IEP meeting during the month of Ramadan on behalf of a Muslim family, who were following the tradition of fasting from dawn to dusk. On entering the designated meeting room, she and the family were shocked (and in the family's case, offended) to see doughnuts sitting on the conference table.

Power Imbalance

By the time Ms. Ologbon reaches the table, it is safe to assume that the IEP team has become dysfunctional to some degree. When schools respond with an attitude that communicates, "Well, all that [bad stuff] happened before, so let's just forget about it," anger is frequently the result. In an effort to restore positive working relationships, Ms. Ologbon strives to "kill with kindness." Sometimes, however, that is not enough to counterbalance the differences in the perceived power of the IEP team members.

As many others have mentioned—the principal (Chapter 1), the general education teacher (Chapter 2), the special education teacher (Chapter 3), the ESOL teacher (Chapter 4), the parent (Chapter 7), the translator (Chapter 8), and the guidance counselor (Chapter 12)—power becomes manifest in an "us versus them" outlook with parents versus teachers, administrators versus parents, and outsiders (like special education attorneys) versus the school. This is especially true in terms of communication and collaboration.

Unclear Communication

For example, Ms. Ologbon believes that IEP meetings with CLD families become adversarial due to lack of information. As she puts it, "90% of problems would be solved if someone would just answer parents' questions." In addition, IEP team members should be judicious and careful with the language they use. For example, the overuse of educational acronyms (such as IEP instead of Individualized Education Program) and idioms can be confusing to families, the translator, and other non-school team members. Using these rather than "spelling out" the formal terms results in a feeling that school-based personnel are "in the know" while CLD families are not, thus underscoring the imbalance of power.

Similarly, CLD families may use language confusing to school personnel. For example, Ms. Ologbon shared a story about a Spanish-speaking parent who used the expression *no tener pelos en la lengua*, the literal translation of which is "not to have hairs on your tongue," which figuratively refers to someone who speaks his mind. The parent and translator understood what was being communicated, but had real difficulty explaining the expression to members of the team who did not speak Spanish.

The Need for Data

Further contributing to ineffective communication are unrealistic expecta-tions. Ms. Ologbon is quick to point out that this is true for all IEP team members. For example, it is often the case that the school underestimates the child's abilities or that the parents overestimate what the school should accomplish in a given school year.

As a result, Ms. Ologbon insists on seeing quantitative data because anecdotal data—while informative in certain situations—is "too soft" to document student progress. However, the school usually cannot provide concrete numbers. As Ms. Ologbon remarks, "I always know that I can catch a school on data."

Ms. Ologbon posits that teachers prefer "stories" over "numbers" because the former are easier to collect and to remember. However, Ms. Ologbon does acknowledge that there can be downsides to quantitative data, the most notable being that the data rather than the child can become the focus of instruction. In such a case, the CLD child is taught in a vacuum just for the sake of "getting the numbers."

Ms. Ologbon also insists on the documentation of "everything" on the Present Level of Performance (or PLOP) page of the IEP. She feels that this provides clarity and continuity for subsequent IEP team members, while also providing a "road map" for the child's academic future. Her favorite question is, "Where do you want to see your child at 22?" However, there is often disagreement among IEP team members as to where that road map should lead, which makes reaching consensus on even the simplest goals more difficult.

That being said, Ms. Ologbon finds that schools are—for the most part—open to input from CLD families and other non-school personnel. They welcome parents' insights and suggestions on the draft IEPs sent home before the meeting and during the meeting itself. Further, she feels that the school is responsive to families as they "move up the chain" to request additional services or accommodations for their child. However, Ms. Ologbon does see several areas in which the IEP process for CLD families could be improved.

SUGGESTIONS FOR IMPROVEMENT

Ms. Ologbon's experience representing the interests of CLD families in IEP meetings leads her to suggest several improvements for the process. These include ensuring that all IEP team members understand the value of special education and cultivate an awareness of students' backgrounds. Further, Ms. Ologbon believes that additional services and resources for those services would also be beneficial.

Highlight the Importance of Special Education

According to Ms. Ologbon, the area most in need of change is school culture (Deal & Peterson, 2016). First and foremost, everyone in the school building needs to view special education as important. The school principal should set the tone that inclusion is a valued part of the school community. Contributing to the problem is the fact that faculty work in silos and rarely interact, much less collaborate, with others in the building. For example, it is uncommon for special education teachers to have regular opportunities to speak with general education teachers and vice versa.

In turn, the lack of collaboration often leads to issues in terms of both instruction and accurate data collection. With regard to the former, when faculty do not have the opportunity to work together to plan effective instruction—especially with regard to differentiation—students' needs may be unmet. With regard to data collection, when special education teachers are not afforded the opportunity to work with general education teachers, there is often confusion about what types of data need to be collected and how often it should be collected, which results in students' needs being misunderstood.

Understand Cultural Diversity

Additional misunderstandings arise when a CLD student exhibits negative behaviors. One teacher might view a student's "acting out" as disruptive, while another might view it as a method for getting attention. As such, Ms. Ologbon believes that it would be best for all IEP team members to be better informed about cultural diversity, which she believes will help them to refrain from making judgments about students and their families. In other words, taking the time to understand families' experiences would result in more positive relationships overall.

As an example, Ms. Ologbon recounts the story of a student who was born in Russia and was adopted by a Russian family in the United States. The student was described by her teachers as "a very difficult child—willful and disrespectful." They assumed that she was "being bad." After this had been shared in the IEP meeting, her adoptive parents explained that the adoption process had been very traumatic for her and that she was undergoing counseling to help with the effects of that trauma. According to Ms. Ologbon, the teachers responded with "Oh well, *that* [the explanation] explains it [the undesirable behaviors]," which prompted her to reflect on the ongoing need for ways to create more understanding among IEP team members.

Specifically, Ms. Ologbon feels that IEP team members need to have more than one way to view a child. It is often the case that students like the one described above are categorized in a binary fashion: good/bad, polite/rude, compliant/noncompliant, and so on. While students are more complex than that, school-based IEP team members have very little (if any) training in post-traumatic stress disorder (PTSD), mental health issues, and/or poverty, all of which have profound effects on any student's ability to learn and to demonstrate that learning, but are even more detrimental for a CLD student (Cartledge, Lo, Vincent, & Robinson-Ervin, 2015).

Increase Resources for Services

Similarly, Ms. Ologbon believes another area in need of improvement is that of resources, especially time and money. In terms of the former, Ms. Ologbon feels that neither the school day in particular nor the academic year in general is conducive to teachers getting to know their CLD students on a personal level.

With regard to the school day, a day in the life of a special education teacher is focused on data collection, managing students on a caseload, and attending IEP meetings. When, as often happens, a special education teacher's caseload is overloaded, it is even harder to take time to get to know her/his students better. With regard to the school year, given the number of people required to be on an IEP team and the number of school holidays, weather-related cancellations, and other impediments, it can take several months to coordinate everyone's schedules.

Ms. Ologbon also believes that schools should be more considerate of a student's native language when sharing resources, communicating between school and home, and documenting progress (Fellin, Desmarais, & Lindsay, 2014). In her experience, CLD families often come to an IEP meeting with little to no advance notice/warning of what to expect. Although they may have received the suggested goals as required by law, the parents' understanding of English might be limited or nonexistent, so they may not have understood the goals. Ms. Ologbon likens this type of situation to being told to drive while wearing a blindfold. Families are thus put in the position of having to trust school professionals, regardless of whether or not that trust is warranted. As Ms. Ologbon puts it, "Language is an issue, but it's what's behind the language that is *the* issue."

QUESTIONS FOR DISCUSSION/REFLECTION

- How important is the disability rights attorney's role in the IEP meetings for CLD students? How does a disability rights attorney's position shape his or her perspectives on the process?
- Do you agree with the idea of treating one's clients or students like one's own children? Why or why not?
- To what extent should school districts make CLD families aware that they could consult with a disability rights attorney?

- What strategies do you employ to avoid or mitigate burnout, disillusionment, and/or exhaustion?
- Describe a time when you experienced a misunderstanding due to a language barrier. In what ways is that experience similar to those discussed in this chapter? In what ways is it different?
- How can expectations for students be more effectively communicated?
- Ms. Ologbon says that IEP meetings with CLD families are complex, both legally and emotionally. What other complexities can you identify?

ADDITIONAL RESOURCES

These articles, books, reports, and/or websites provide more information about the topics mentioned in this chapter.

Disability Rights

A Guide to Disability Rights Laws: https://www.ada.gov/cguide.htm
American Bar Association Commission on Mental and Physical Disability Law: http://www.abanet.org
Disability Rights International: https://www.driadvocacy.org
National Disability Rights Network: http://www.ndrn.org/index.php

Intercultural Communication

Neuliep, J. (2017). *Intercultural communication: A contextual approach.* Washington, DC: SAGE Publications.
Novinger, T. (2013). *Intercultural communication: A practical guide.* Austin: University of Texas Press.
Piller, I. (2011). *Intercultural communication: A critical introduction.* Edinburgh: Edinburgh University Press.

Due Process

IDEA Special Education Due Process Complaints/Hearing Requests: A Guide for Parents and Youth. (2014). Retrieved from https://www.cadreworks.org/sites/default/files/resources/DueProcessParentGuide_FINAL_10.24.14_0.pdf
Osborne, A. G., & Russo, C. J. (2014). *Special education and the law: A guide for practitioners.* Thousand Oaks, CA: Corwin Press.
Understanding Due Process: http://www.understandingspecialeducation.com/IEP-due-process.html
Wrightslaw: http://www.wrightslaw.com/info/dp.index.htm

Chapter Seven

The Parent's Voice

"It is always embattled, you know?"

Parents have many roles in an Individualized Education Program (IEP) meeting. One is to participate as team members in the creation of the narrative on their child's Present Level of Performance (PLOP). Given that they know best how their children learn and interact with others, albeit not in a school setting, another role that parents serve is as advocates for their child. A third role is to contribute to the development of IEP goals for their child. Parents have extensive rights, though they are not always aware of this and may participate at varying levels of involvement. For example, parents have the right to disagree with an IEP if their input is not considered, and they do not have to sign an IEP with which they are not in agreement.

Ms. Tark is the mother of David, an 11-year-old boy with Down syndrome and sensory processing issues. Ms. Tark is a native speaker of Spanish, and her husband is a native speaker of Tagalog. Both are also fluent in English. The extended family includes speakers of both Tagalog and Spanish, and David has been consistently exposed to multilingualism throughout his life. Ms. Tark holds a graduate degree in the field of communications from a well-regarded university, and she works in a professional setting using this degree.

During her interview, Ms. Tark discussed her experiences dealing with two public school settings: a medium-sized school system in a relatively affluent suburban district and an urban charter school. Ms. Tark started the discussion by explaining the diagnosis and early intervention efforts for David, her efforts to ensure a bilingual education for him, and her interactions with educators and administrators in school settings. In addition, she talked

57

about her larger efforts to engage in self-education and community relations in order to ensure the best possible educational experience for David.

Since David's diagnosis shortly after his birth in 2003, Ms. Tark has been engaged in seeking and managing services for him. In the beginning, she initiated early intervention, and he received services at home, including speech therapy. Later, she enrolled him in a private preschool that had expressed willingness and the ability to accommodate his needs. When it came time for kindergarten, Ms. Tark enrolled David in her local public school. Only after enormous frustration did her search for alternatives lead her to a new charter school in a different school district where he is currently a student.

This chapter focuses on Ms. Tark's experiences navigating early intervention and the public school setting and the IEP process, as well as the challenges she faced framed as suggestions for improving the IEP process. Ms. Tark has been an activist parent and has educated herself in order to overcome obstacles in obtaining optimal educational services for her son. As a result, she has participated in the special education process from a position that is more empowered than many of the culturally and linguistically diverse (CLD) parents described by professionals in other chapters. Nevertheless, she has encountered many of the same issues.

PERSPECTIVES ON CULTURAL AND LINGUISTIC DIVERSITY

Ms. Tark's experiences with issues surrounding cultural and linguistic diversity have primarily concentrated on finding acceptance of her son's multilingualism, an issue that arose in the context of early intervention. From the time David was a baby, she has spoken to him only in Spanish (her first language) during the day; when her husband returns in the evenings, he speaks to David in English. While his father's first language is Tagalog, and their son has been exposed to Tagalog through interactions with his paternal grandparents, Mr. Tark believes that English will be far more useful for him. Ms. Tark notes that although David was language delayed when young, he had mastered numerous sight words by age three and could respond to signing in Spanish or English.

Multilingualism

The first county-provided speech therapist with whom the Tark family worked encouraged the family to stop speaking Spanish and other languages to David so that he could learn English. Feeling that this was wrong for David culturally, emotionally, and even developmentally, Ms. Tark resisted. It was this encounter that started Ms. Tark's process of research and education in the field of Down syndrome education.

As a result of her investigation, she unearthed numerous research studies of children with Down syndrome who speak two or more languages due to their parents' backgrounds; these children were able to differentiate between languages, as is the case for typically developing bilingual peers. As a result of this research, Ms. Tark felt confident that multilingualism would not be a problem for David based on his early experiences with Spanish and English, along with exposure to Tagalog. Moreover, she also believed that supporting his multilingualism was essential for his identity in the family. Nevertheless, her research did not convince the first speech therapist, and the issue remained an unresolved source of conflict.

The issue arose again when David entered the public school system and was placed in a self-contained special education program. Ms. Tark requested that David be mainstreamed and included in a bilingual classroom. She said David and the teacher in that classroom responded positively when the school did a trial placement, and that the teacher was very dedicated, really liked David, and was very happy to have him in her classroom.

The teacher was teaching him to read in Spanish, which was easier for him than trying to read in English. Although Ms. Tark wanted David to continue in the bilingual program, at the end of the year, the school would not allow David to do so, stating that his services could be better delivered in a single-language setting. She did not agree, but felt unable to resist their decision.

Several years later, when Ms. Tark left that school district in favor of another district's charter school, which she had undertaken extensive efforts to find, she found the linguistic—as well as special education—solution to her quest. The charter school has been able to provide the special education services needed in the context of a bilingual classroom. They view his bilingualism as a way to reach him, to connect school to home life, and are continuing his education in both Spanish and English.

PERSPECTIVES ON THE IEP MEETING

Ms. Tark frames her perspectives within the broader context of her son's education. These broad experiences inform her views on the dynamics of IEP meetings themselves.

Experiences with Special Education

In spite of the initial difficulties with the county speech therapist rejecting the appropriateness of a bilingual environment, Ms. Tark's overall experiences with early intervention education was positive. However, transitioning from early intervention services, where providers visited her home and provided extensive information in the preschool setting, to the larger and more ritualized environment of the local elementary school proved to be a shock. Ms. Tark felt isolated on numerous levels.

First, she felt that her son was excluded from the larger school community. Special education students had a separate entrance to the school and different morning procedures from the rest of the students. In terms of relationships within the school community, both among parents and between parents and the school, Ms. Tark encountered a dramatic shift toward isolation.

In terms of participating in her son's education and school life, she was suddenly shut out and unwelcome in the second kindergarten classroom, following her son's exit from the bilingual program. Finally, the lack of information, both from teachers and specialist service providers, was the most frustrating issue she faced.

IEP Dynamics and Services

During her son's years of early intervention, once she moved beyond the speech therapist who opposed multilingualism, Ms. Tark generally had a positive experience about IEP meetings. She found her caseworker to be a champion who really battled for David's rights, particularly in the preschool setting. As a result, she had what she termed a "wonderful" relationship with district officials and very smooth IEP meetings, including her transition meeting in preparation for kindergarten, in which the school district agreed to the mainstream bilingual class that supported his language development and home environment.

Once she arrived at the elementary school and began her IEP meetings in that setting, however, the lack of communication led to distrust. In spite of a great relationship with the bilingual kindergarten teacher, once the school ended that placement, the process and dynamics became "embattled" and this dynamic persisted through second grade for several reasons.

First, because the decision to take her son out of the bilingual class was based on the special education teacher's needs rather than her son's, she felt that the school was trying to fit him into their structural model rather than tailoring the services to meet her son's needs.

In addition to the class placement, she saw the same pattern in his daily routines and services. She wanted him to walk through the front door of the school and walk to his classroom like all the other students. However, the school wanted him to take the special education bus, enter the school through a separate door designated for special education students, and sit in the cafeteria with all the other special education students. She felt strongly that, due to his diagnosis, the school was limiting his options and eliminating the possibility of David interacting with typically developing peers due to the school's prescribed steps and routines.

Another struggle Ms. Tark had with the school was in obtaining appropriate accommodations for her son's sensory regulation needs. She had requested an occupational therapy (OT) evaluation, but the school determined that there was no need. She then returned to her private provider, who sent her to a diagnostic center for a full OT evaluation. The OT found significant sensory processing issues and recommended 15-minute sensory processing breaks every hour, an accommodation the school was unwilling to make.

She experienced similar difficulty in obtaining physical therapy (PT) services for her son, although he had received PT services throughout early intervention and still had numerous balance and midline issues. In numerous IEP meetings across several years, she raised this need but was told that because he was ambulatory, "He can walk. He won't get PT, period."

Perhaps most significantly, before the IEP meeting that would determine his first-grade placement, the new teacher told her that the son's kindergarten placement would have to last two years. Ms. Tark approached the district's director of special education about the matter, and he told her that was not the case. As a result, she invited him to her next IEP meeting, when her son's placement would be discussed.

In the meeting that the director attended, there was dialogue and progress. Everyone was polite and civil. Because the speech goals were written as behavior goals, the director wanted them rewritten so that they could proceed to sign the IEP. However, the speech therapist was not in attendance, so the meeting had to be continued at a later date.

When Ms. Tark arrived for the next meeting, which the director could not attend, she noticed that there was lipstick on coffee cups and that those cups were half empty, evidence that the "meeting before the meeting" had taken place. It was evident to her that the group had decided in advance that they were going to retain David in kindergarten, in spite of statements to the contrary in the previous meeting.

Because the district's director of special education was not in attendance, the school's framework position had changed from, "He's moving on to first grade with these supports," to "No, we need to retain him another year because it's not appropriate for him to move on." Ms. Tark lost the battle in that meeting, and her son repeated kindergarten.

Ms. Tark's final disagreement with the school system was over her son's academic progress, particularly in reading. She requested that phonemic awareness be added to David's IEP goals, but the school responded that he had been placed in reading intervention based on an assessment by the reading specialist. When she asked for more information about the assessment, including how and why he answered certain questions and how the intervention in question was selected, they produced a minimal checklist that essentially indicated that "he won't answer questions; just put him at the lowest level."

Ms. Tark's questions about whether the reading intervention aligned with his IEP goals were never answered. Instead, she was told that her expectations needed to be readjusted and that she needed to accept that David was not going to read at the same level as anyone else or may not read at all. This "us versus them" dynamic has frequently arisen in discussions with others interviewed: the principal (Chapter 1), the general education teacher (Chapter 2), the special education teacher (Chapter 3), the ESOL teacher (Chapter 4), the advocate (Chapter 5), the translator (Chapter 8), and the guidance counselor (Chapter 12).

System-Oriented Services and Success Rates

Because of her interest and research in special education, Ms. Tark eventually gained a position in the district's parent resource center (PRC), a venue for educating parents of children with special needs and IEPs. From this vantage point, she gained a firsthand look at special education services in the district more broadly, continued to learn about the school system, and advised other parents extensively. She also uncovered information that she found troubling regarding the IEP process. She discovered numerous IEPs with the same boilerplate language, and even some mistaken names, indicating direct copying and pasting from one IEP to another.

She said, "I understand people are busy, and I understand that you wanna take shortcuts, and if things have worked with one child, it could possibly work with another child, but being a parent, you really want to know that your IEP is individualized." For her, this confirmed her own experiences that the special education services in the district were system-centered rather than student-centered.

Another aspect of her learning in the resource center led her to access district statistics. The outcomes for special education were so dismal that she began to consider homeschooling David or placing him in a neighboring district. After extensive efforts, David was selected for a spot in an urban special education–oriented charter school in a nearby district. The director had founded the school to serve children with special needs, having discovered a dearth of truly responsive services for children with learning challenges and differences. Although this entailed moving from the suburbs to the city, in Ms. Tark's estimation, it was well worth the effort.

SUGGESTIONS FOR IMPROVEMENT

Many of Ms. Tark's experiences with her local school district raise issues related to honesty, respect, setting high expectations, and engaging in dialogue and partnership with families. These experiences are the basis of her suggestions for improvement. Her recommendations relate to parent expectations, how meetings should be scheduled, and considering alternatives when discussing a student's least restrictive environment.

Partner with Families

Ms. Tark's description of her relationship with the urban charter school reflects respect for students and parents, honesty and trust and open communications, setting high expectations for students, and providing appropriate, individualized special education services in the least restrictive environment. These experiences with the urban public charter school have been so positive that they provide a road map for improvement of the special education she experienced in her neighborhood school district.

Although the charter school experienced some start-up issues, Ms. Tark has been very happy with its communication, inclusiveness, level of attention, and accommodations. She was impressed that the teachers and specialists involved had actually read his IEP and evaluation reports and used these to determine placement and services that would help him transition to the school and thrive there.

When he entered the new school, David was evaluated and discovered to be two years behind. Since then, he has made rapid progress. Within a year, he managed to catch up on first- and second-grade work and his current grade level; she said that he was motivated to learn, a behavior which was absent in his neighborhood school before. She said that IEP meetings are collaborative and that the school recognizes her son's needs and has provided the necessary supports; she has not needed to undertake a battle to receive them.

Explore Educational Alternatives

Ms. Tark was elated to report that David is treated with respect, included in classroom activities, allowed to be with typically developing peers, and has friends for the first time. She said that she feels that he is in a safe environment with many supports in place. The new school has taken into consideration the larger family values and identity and is encouraging her son's bilingualism, a fact which seems to make both Ms. Tark and her son very happy. Further, unlike the local school district where David began his education, the charter school acknowledged his sensory needs from the outset. At the beginning of the day, he goes to the sensory room so that he starts the school day well-regulated and ready to learn in his classroom.

The approach of Ms. Tark's charter school seems to provide a template for key areas of successful planning and delivery of special education services, based on individualized education plans that are set up to promote a student's development and maximize his potential. If special education programs are to achieve the best results for students and families, providing this kind of foundation for family-school cooperation in the interest of students is essential.

On a national level, there is emerging discussion of the role of charter schools in special education. Currently, there is a slight increase in enrollments and higher levels of inclusion in mainstream classrooms (Rim & Kothari, 2018). Other groups, however, note that some charter schools struggle to accommodate special education students. Because the Individuals with Disabilities Education Act (IDEA) mandates that publicly funded charters offer the same services as local education agencies, these schools require additional investment to adequately serve these students (Mulligan, 2011).

QUESTIONS FOR DISCUSSION AND REFLECTION

- How important is the parent's role in the IEP meetings for CLD students? How does a parent's position shape his or her perspectives on the process?
- Why do some professionals consider bilingual education a barrier for students with special needs? Do you agree or disagree?
- Ms. Tark felt excluded from the school community when her son left the bilingual class; what can schools do to build parent participation?
- To what extent should institutional resources impact what is a "least restrictive environment" in a given setting?
- Based on your experiences, do you think that parental expectations are often too high for their children? Why or why not?
- Ms. Tark mentions seeing language taken from one student's IEP copied and pasted into another's. Have you seen others taking shortcuts?
- Are charter schools with special missions a good solution for educating exceptional children? Why or why not?

ADDITIONAL RESOURCES

These articles, books, reports, and/or websites provide more information about the topics mentioned in this chapter.

Respect for Students

Alter, M., Gottlieb, M., & Gottlieb, J. (2018). Four ways schools fail special education students. *Education Week*. Retrieved from https://www.edweek.org/ew/articles/2018/02/15/four-ways-schools-fail-special-education-students.html

Cohen, J., Cardillo, R., & Pickeral, T. (2011). Creating a climate of respect. *Education Leadership, 69.* Retrieved from http://www.ascd.org/publications/educational-leadership/sept11/vol69/num01/Creating-a-Climate-of-Respect.aspx

Milsom, A. (n.d.). Creating positive school experiences for students with disabilities. Retrieved from http://www.readingrockets.org/article/creating-positive-school-experiences-students-disabilities

Multilingualism and Students with Special Needs

Grosjean, F. (2017). Supporting bilingual children with special education needs. *Psychology Today,* January 18. Retrieved from https://www.psychologytoday.com/us/blog/life-bilingual/201701/supporting-bilingual-children-special-education-needs

Morrison, D. (2007, July). Children with Down syndrome can become multilingual. *Dalhousie University News*. Retrieved from https://www.dal.ca/news/2007/07/12/bird.html

Wright, J. (2012, October). Cognition and behavior: Bilingualism aids people with autism. *Spectrum*. Retrieved from https://www.spectrumnews.org/news/cognition-and-behavior-bilingualism-aids-people-with-autism/

Least Restrictive Environment (LRE)

Center for Parent Information and Resources (2017). *Considering LRE in Placement Decisions.* Retrieved from http://www.parentcenterhub.org/placement-lre/

Morin, A. (n.d.). *Least restrictive environment (LRE): What you need to know.* Retrieved from https://www.understood.org/en/school-learning/special-services/special-education-basics/least-restrictive-environment-lre-what-you-need-to-know

Wrightslaw (n.d.). Questions and answers on least restrictive environment (LRE) requirements of the IDEA. Retrieved from http://www.wrightslaw.com/info/lre.osers.memo.idea.htm

Charter Schools for Students with Special Needs

Ahearn, E. M. (2002). *Charter schools and special education: A report on state policies.* Discover IDEA. Retrieved from https://www.cesa7.org/sped/discoveridea/topdocs/spec_ed_policies.htm

Chapter Eight

The Translator's Voice

"Translation is a moral responsibility."

In Individualized Education Program (IEP) meetings, the role of the interpreter is to provide a linguistic "bridge" between school officials and culturally and linguistically diverse (CLD) parents to ensure that communication from both sides is available to the other. The reauthorization of the Individuals with Disabilities Education Act (IDEA) in 1997 stipulated that schools must ensure that parents understand the IEP meeting proceedings, and that notices must be written in understandable language and provided in the native language unless it is not feasible to do so (U.S. Department of Education, 2016; Minnesota Department of Education, 2005, pp. 117–118). While a translator is someone who translates written documents, an interpreter translates verbal interaction.[1] In school district parlance, the term "translator" refers to someone who provides both written and verbal translation, and so we will use that term here.

In addition to these roles, some states and school districts recommend including a person who serves as a cultural mediator, although there are no data on which states or districts do so. One state defines this person as someone knowledgeable about special education policy and procedures as well as someone with links to the cultural community being served (Colorado Department of Education, 2015, p. 1). In many locales, this cultural mediation seems to be undertaken informally and voluntarily by teachers or liaisons who understand the culture of CLD families and are able to understand their needs and perspectives. Ms. Bolcs falls into this category, providing interpretation, translation, and cultural outreach services.

Ms. Bolcs has been a translator in her school district for 24 years and has sat in thousands of IEP meetings at the middle school level. She began this

work as a volunteer when her own daughter was referred for special education services. After her daughter graduated, Ms. Bolcs continued to help the
school interact with other non-English-speaking families and became the
parent liaison at the school, where she has worked ever since. She is bilingual
in Spanish and English.

Although she has no training in interpretation or special education, Ms.
Bolcs has leveraged her experience in IEP meetings to provide explanations
of services and IEP policies to the parents with whom she works. She noted
that, years ago, the school district had formal interpreters, but now the burden
falls on staff like her. As a result, she feels a moral responsibility to translate
an IEP to the best of her ability and to explain it thoroughly to parents.
Nearing retirement, she is concerned about her replacement, because "the
new girls don't even speak good Spanish."

PERSPECTIVES ON CULTURAL AND LINGUISTIC DIVERSITY

Ms. Bolcs's work in education is focused on bridging the divide between
home and school and in the context of IEP meetings. She has deep insights
and experiences on how cultural and linguistic differences impact educational processes and outcomes for students.

Family Culture and Impact on Services

Differences between home culture and school culture create the possibility of
misunderstandings and problems for CLD parents and students alike. In the
case of parents, their view of schools is shaped by the norms in their home
countries. The norms of U.S. schools may differ. For example, in many home
countries, Ms. Bolcs says, students are placed in classes based on their level
of knowledge; in the United States, grade-level placements are largely determined by age. This may create a perception among parents that their children
are advancing (unless they must repeat a grade), when in fact they are not.
On the other hand, for recent arrivals, home country grade levels may not
correspond to U.S. grade levels, so parents may believe their children are
doing poorly if they enter a lower grade than that completed in their home
country.

In addition, parents themselves may come from rural areas, where they
have spent their lives working in fields, and have no experience of formal
education at all. Thus they have no point of reference for understanding
curriculum, educational processes, and the role of teachers and administrators. There may be even greater respect for the authority of the school from
those parents who do have some educational experience, and thus they view
the school with deference and do not participate in school life, teacher meetings, or other school-based activities. This creates an impression, in turn, at

the school that parents are uninvolved and indifferent, even though that is rarely the case.

Cultural differences may also impact students directly. As will be discussed later in this chapter, CLD students are more likely to be referred for discipline or testing, particularly for emotional issues. Some of these problems, however, may be culturally rooted. For example, Ms. Bolcs believes that Latin cultures are more emotional and expressive. This may create the impression of students who are overly reactive.

In another example, she notes that "We [Salvadorans] always smile." If the teacher calls on the student and the student smiles rather than answer a question, teachers may see this as a sign of disrespect and respond, "There is nothing to smile about." They may even impose a disciplinary penalty. When students smile during detention, it is interpreted as not taking the punishment seriously, which could anger teachers or administrators.

School Culture and Impact on Services

The first area where cultural and linguistic diversity issues intersect with special education processes is at the level of teachers and classrooms. Ms. Bolcs believes that many students who are referred for evaluation do not need special education services. Due to cultural differences and sometimes low expectations, teachers may consider some CLD students a disruption in class. "Minority students are easier to punish," she says, because parents do not protest or involve lawyers.

She believes some teachers want to get rid of kids who are problematic and label them as delayed or as having an emotional disturbance (ED). If a child is not paying attention in class, he may be tested for emotional problems. Some students are put into life skills (rather than academic) programs, although they may not need these classes. Teachers are often confused and think that language is the reason students are behind and that their home country education is poor. Most commonly, "minorities" are labeled as having an ED or a learning disability (LD) rather than other disability categories.

On another level, a conflicting dynamic is in play. Ten years ago, Ms. Bolcs's district was audited for overclassification of "minority students" in special education. Schools are under pressure to avoid this phenomenon, so they sometimes prefer to minimize evaluations and special education placements. According to Ms. Bolcs, it is easier to get out of special education now that parents can sign a form and refuse services.

Although schools do not consciously take advantage of parents' lack of empowerment and advocacy, they *do* wish to avoid overclassification. Ms. Bolcs also notes that 504 plans—for other health impairments—are becoming more commonly used instead of IEPs. Interestingly, even Ms. Bolcs holds the (mis)understanding that schools cannot refer CLD students for special education services until five years have elapsed.

Lastly, Ms. Bolcs has seen a great deal of implicit bias in the way that school personnel interact with minority parents versus white parents. Even in the case of well-educated CLD parents—whose participation in IEP meetings is quite different from their less educated counterparts—Ms. Bolcs has observed that the school is very paternalistic toward Latino parents.

School Improvements

Taking a long view, the focus of schools on the issue of overclassification combined with the reforms of the past 15 years regarding minority education in general has resulted in improvements in the education of CLD students. Due to the accountability resulting from the No Child Left Behind Act of 2001 (No Child Left Behind [NCLB], 2002), schools are more focused on minority and special education students than in the past because these students must pass standardized tests, with those test scores available to parents and the general public. In addition, teachers can see that, based on test scores, students *have* mastered curriculum and, in some cases, they can exit special education and return to mainstream classrooms.

However, Ms. Bolcs believes that not all the news is bad with regard to CLD students and special education. In spite of the biases noted above, she reports that school officials do respect parents from all ethnicities and educational backgrounds. Many general education teachers do advocate for their CLD students, and there are now more English for Speakers of Other Languages (ESOL) teachers designated for dually identified students. Finally, some special education administrators from the central office are very skilled at working effectively with CLD families.

PERSPECTIVES ON THE IEP MEETING

As the principal (Chapter 1), the general education teacher (Chapter 2), the English for ESOL teacher (Chapter 4), and the guidance counselor (Chapter 12) have expressed, Ms. Bolcs believes that the role of the translator is influenced heavily by meeting dynamics. She also explains the numerous ways that cultural and linguistic diversity create additional challenges for parents participating in IEP meetings.

Meeting Dynamics

In Ms. Bolcs's role of translator at IEP meetings, she has seen numerous dynamics at work. Regarding her own role, she feels empowered to provide additional explanation beyond mere translation of words to the meaning that lies behind them. The non-Spanish-speaking people at the table do ask what she is saying, but she has never been limited in what she could say. While she does attempt to explain the IEP content, it is always while attempting to digest it herself.

In only one case in all of her years working with CLD parents and IEP meetings has a teacher called the parents herself and given Ms. Bolcs a copy of the IEP in advance so she could become familiar with it prior to the meeting. Moreover, teachers do not discuss the IEP or student needs with her in advance so she, like the parents, is attempting to process the contents rapidly during the meeting.

In Ms. Bolcs's observations, parents' background education plays an enormous role in how meetings unfold, much more than do language and culture. She believes that the school reacts differently to well-educated CLD parents such as those from international business, government, or other professional backgrounds. CLD parents with a high level of education in their home country do research, find out about options for education and services, and come to meetings well prepared. They know how to advocate for their children and when to ask questions. When these parents come to meetings, schools are much more careful and respectful in their language and demeanor. Meetings take two and a half hours rather than the half hour allotted for IEP meetings with parents lacking in significant formal education. The well-educated CLD parents are very well informed, able to participate in meetings, and are satisfied with the services provided as a result.

Barriers to Parent Participation

One of the greatest obstacles to parent participation is a simple lack of understanding of the special education process. According to Ms. Bolcs, most CLD parents do not even know what special education is. Often they hear the word "special" and think it is something good. With these parents, prior to the meeting Ms. Bolcs tries to explain what special education is. She says that parents try to understand but, in many cases, they do not have the background knowledge to do so. She also notes that it is very difficult to translate and explain many of the concepts during a meeting. The language and approaches are specialized and complex, the time allotted is limited, and the document itself is quite complicated.

On one hand, Ms. Bolcs becomes frustrated with parents when she spends a great deal of effort to ensure their participation and they fail to engage. If the school offers workshops, the parents simply do not attend. If the school asks them to sign, and she thinks they should perhaps raise questions or issues, she asks them repeatedly for their input in an effort to have them participate. Usually, though, they demur or shrug their shoulders. Ms. Bolcs knows that if the parents ask for more services, their children will benefit, but this is simply not part of their culture.

One of Ms. Bolcs's greatest disappointments is that, even when parents *do* understand the process and available services and their rights, sometimes they simply fail to advocate. In one case, she had participated in IEP meetings for a deaf student throughout her time at the middle school. Both she and the child's teacher had been active advocates and had helped the parents access appropriate services in the program for students who are deaf and hard of hearing.

At the meeting for preparing a transition to high school, however, they learned that the high school did not offer such a program. Ms. Bolcs and the teacher discussed the possibility of a private school placement since the district could not accommodate the student appropriately at the high school level. Unfortunately, the parents instead agreed to placement in a self-contained special education classroom despite the fact that, other than her hearing impairment, the student had no difficulties whatsoever in accessing the curriculum.

Ms. Bolcs feels that parents should pay more attention due to the overrepresentation of minorities in special education, but she recognizes the reasons why parents do not push or question the school. First, it is not part of their cultural background; schools are viewed with the utmost respect and as authority. Also, she says, CLD parents have many issues with which to contend. Many lack documentation regarding their immigrant status, and they are afraid that they do not have the right to argue for fear of running afoul of the legal system. Many CLD parents are working multiple jobs and are in precarious economic situations. The problem that results is the school assumes that, with translation, parents understand, when in fact they do not.

SUGGESTIONS FOR IMPROVEMENT

When it comes to CLD families and special education, the discussion with Ms. Bolcs provides numerous areas for improvement for school and parent involvement. She believes there is a particular need for changes in how IEP meetings are planned and conducted, schools' cultural responsiveness, teachers' approaches to student needs, and parents' involvement in their children's education.

Include Parents in IEP Meeting Dynamics

In planning and preparing for IEP meetings with CLD families, the experiences of Ms. Bolcs reveal ways in which preparations could be broader to ensure more equitable parent involvement. First and foremost, parents need to be participants in deciding meeting times. Ms. Bolcs mentioned in passing that some parents cannot attend due to their work schedules. Allowing them to provide input on possible days and times could mitigate this problem to some extent.

While it is true that some parents work multiple jobs and are unable to take off during school hours or at the time a team can meet, giving parents a voice in negotiation would likely improve their involvement. Additionally, due to the assumption that parents cannot (or will not) attend, sometimes IEPs are sent home to be signed without an actual meeting taking place. Because the documents go home in English—and a highly technical English at that—the gap between parents and their children's special education only widens.

It also seems that, even though in some cases Ms. Bolcs calls parents prior to the meeting to explain the meeting's purpose, the parents would also benefit from hearing from the teachers themselves. She believes that teachers should call before the meeting to make sure parents understand what an IEP is and what special education entails, and the reasons they believe the child could benefit from additional support to meet his or her educational goals. This kind of contact, ideally, should be ongoing.

Ms. Bolcs raised the issue that, during the meetings, the IEP team needs to allot more time and then take that time to explain the educational needs and possible remedies to parents. All too often, schools schedule a minimal amount of time, and parents remain passive throughout. In order to support parents' involvement, meeting participants should offer parents options—not just the option to agree or disagree with their approaches—and ask them which option they think would work best for their child. In this way, parents could feel empowered as participants in their child's education.

Change School Culture

Ms. Bolcs had strong recommendations for school improvements, many of which are difficult to measure or to implement. Granted, these improvements may be part of existing mission statements, but the on-the-ground reality often falls far short of the stated ideals.

First, Ms. Bolcs noted that schools need to do their best for children, something that is not happening now. As she noted, not all students can be evaluated in the same way or considered by the same standards. When CLD students are measured according to standards that do not necessarily take diversity into account, their performance can be negatively affected, which in turn causes teachers to lower their expectations for those children's success. In Ms. Bolcs's view, generally speaking, expectations for CLD students are low. Ms. Bolcs feels that students live up[2] to these expectations, a belief that is supported by research (e.g., Gershenson, Holt, & Papageorge, 2016).

Next, Ms. Bolcs stated strongly that leadership on cultural competence must come from the top. While schools may appear to be doing a lot for cultural inclusion, she finds that their efforts are very paternalistic, especially toward Latinos, whether educated or not. In other words, schools need to move beyond this discrimination and treat children as individuals. The superficial aspects of multiculturalism that are adopted by schools, such as the "Heroes and Holidays" approach, do not often address the deeper issues of cultural differences, so more concrete steps should be implemented to achieve true cultural competence (Banks, 2001; Banks, 1993 cited in Chiariello, 2014).

Help Teachers Understand Special Education and CLD

There are also improvements that teachers could make in terms of alleviating the problem of overrepresentation while simultaneously increasing the understanding of students' needs. For example, Ms. Bolcs believes that it would be better if teachers tried different techniques before referring students, so that they have a sense of what works and what does not. She believes that there are students that need more attention, and if teachers could teach in a different way, the students would be fine. She wonders, "How can you not teach a child to read and then report that he is delayed?"

In the cultural domain, as with the school overall, teachers need to develop cultural competence. On the broadest level, Ms. Bolcs believes that teachers need training in how to consider "the whole child." Teachers too often operate from their own frame of reference—a middle-class one—and do not consider whether there are resources at home, whether a child is living in fear of his own or his parents' deportation, whether he is coming to school hungry, or whether there are other intervening life issues.

Encourage Parents to Be More Active

Unlike some in the educational reform community who attribute failures to bridge cultural differences exclusively to school officials, Ms. Bolcs also strongly recommends that parents learn about their children's education. School districts offer workshops, for example, but parents who need the information fail to attend. While she notes that workshops could and should be offered in individual schools, she places the responsibility to participate directly at the feet of the parents. Attending these is a critical first step toward direct involvement in their children's education. Parents should learn to ask questions, she says, and parents need to advocate for their children because this is critical to accessing the necessary special education resources.

QUESTIONS FOR DISCUSSION/REFLECTION

- How important is the translator's role in the IEP meetings for CLD students? How does a translator's position shape his or her perspectives on the process?
- How valid is the need for training of translators which emerges from Ms. Bolcs's comments?
- Do you consider her a balanced intermediary fulfilling the role of translation and cultural mediation? Why or why not?
- How do you think others perceive her role? Parents? Colleagues? Administrators? Others?
- What are some other reasons—besides those posited by Ms. Bolcs—that parents may take the positions they do?
- Based on your own experiences, do you agree that schools continue to hold implicit biases toward groups of parents? Why or why not?
- How can schools do more to involve parents experiencing challenges in participating in their children's education?

NOTES

1. Although a translator is someone who translates written documents and an interpreter translates verbal interaction, in the school contexts we encountered, the word "translator" is commonly used to refer to the person providing interpretation in IEP meetings.

2. It might be more accurate to say "live down."

ADDITIONAL RESOURCES

These articles, books, reports, and/or websites provide more information about the topics mentioned in this chapter.

CLD Students and Special Education

Barrio, B. L. (2015). Fueling disproportionality of culturally and linguistically diverse students in special education: Implications for teacher education programs. *Journal of Mestizo and Indigenous Voices, 1,* 2–9.

Harry, B., & Klingner, J. (2014). *Why are so many minority students in special education?* New York: Teachers College Press.

Hoover, J. J., & deBettencourt, L. U. (2017). Educating culturally and linguistically diverse exceptional learners: The need for continued advocacy. *Exceptionality, 26*(3), 176–189. https://10.1080/09362835.2017.1299530

Translation and Interpretation and Special Education

Cultural mediators, translators, and interpreters. (2015). Colorado Department of Education. Retrieved from http://www.cde.state.co.us/cdesped/ta_culturalmediators

Refugee children in U.S. Schools: A toolkit for teachers and school personnel. (n.d.) Building Refugee Youth and Children's Services. Retrieved from http://www.brycs.org/documents/upload/Interpretation-Translation-FAQ.pdf

Teacher Expectations and Student Achievement

Chu, S-Y. (2011). Teacher efficacy beliefs toward serving culturally and linguistically diverse *students* in special education: Implications of a pilot study. *Education and Urban Society, 45*(3), pp. 385–410.

Papageorge, N., & Gershenson, S. (2016). *Do teacher expectations matter?* Brookings Institution, September 16. Retrieved from https://www.brookings.edu/blog/brown-center-chalkboard/2016/09/16/do-teacher-expectations-matter/

Chapter Nine

The School Psychologist's Voice

"There are lots of pieces to think about."

Although not required by federal law, a school psychologist is often present in Individualized Education Program (IEP) meetings. As part of the IEP team, the school psychologist can make recommendations for assessments, ensure that those assessments are conducted appropriately, analyze the data collected, and/or share the data with the other team members. Further, the school psychologist ensures that the results included in the summary reports are considered as the team writes IEP goals, objectives, or behavior plans.

The school psychologist we interviewed, Ms. Wijaksana, has worked in the K–12 field for nearly 20 years. After beginning her postgraduate studies as a clinical psychologist, she decided to become a school psychologist instead because it was more "optimistic" than what she had observed in her externships in psychiatric hospitals. She has worked in a variety of school settings primarily as a part of a diagnostic staff administering assessments, but has also facilitated social skills groups, offered guidance on 504 plans, and provided individual counseling for students.

Ms. Wijaksana's work with culturally and linguistically diverse (CLD) students has provided her with many insights about this population. Further, since she is not based in a classroom, Ms. Wijaksana has the unique opportunity to view a family's interactions with a school and its teachers from a more removed perspective.

She believes that everyone wants to help the child who is culturally and linguistically diverse, but that lack of understanding and trust—on both sides—often impedes progress. Ms. Wijaksana acknowledges that the heightened emotions (both positive and negative) of an IEP meeting are understandable. Everyone present has a personal interest in the child, but this personal interest can sometimes lead to defensiveness.

PERSPECTIVES ON CULTURAL AND LINGUISTIC DIVERSITY

Ms. Wijaksana reports that the school and district in which she works values research-based best practices and how they relate to educational, psychological, or behavioral assessments for CLD students. However, she also acknowledges the limitations of this approach.

Limitations

For one, she perceives that the research on which the district's best practices are based focuses primarily on students who are Hispanic. As she puts it, "We do the best we can with what we have, but how can we be sure that what we have is the best for the students with whom we're working?"

Another limitation with regard to whether or not a student's needs are being met is also reflected in how the school and district share information with families of CLD students. For example, the district has a handout that lists the community services available to students and their families. The handout is available in hard copy in both English and Spanish at every school in the district. An electronic version of the handout in several different languages is also available, but only through the district's website.

However, information on accessing these resources is provided only in English (i.e., "See this website"), which limits families' access. Thus, while Ms. Wijaksana says that her school is "a welcoming place" overall for CLD families, she feels frustrated when outreach efforts fall short because the relationship between the family and the school is negatively affected when families feel they are being overlooked or forgotten. As a result, many CLD families might not trust the school. Thus, another limitation noted by Ms. Wijaksana is the lack of information which results in a breakdown of relationships between the school and the family.

For example, when registering a child for school, families are asked to indicate the language(s) spoken at home. Ms. Wijaksana reports that parents often say that English is their primary language when in fact it is not. There are many reasons for this. The family might not know for what purpose(s) the question is being asked, or they might not want others to know that they don't speak English. When school representatives discover the discrepancy between what has been reported and what is actually the case, Ms. Wijaksana says that teachers, counselors, and administrators become frustrated at what they perceive to be dishonesty. This in turn affects how they interact with the families, making comments like, "Well, who knows what the truth is with these folks?"

Circumstances like this lead Ms. Wijaksana to lament the lack of understanding of other cultures, which has been pervasive in every school where she has worked. Her training as a school psychologist included only one course in multiculturalism, and it focused more on students with special needs than on students who come from culturally and linguistically diverse backgrounds.

Without a deeper understanding of culture and all it encompasses, Ms. Wijaksana believes, teachers often conflate the differences between a language issue and a disability, thus limiting their ability to understand how language and culture affect a child's development. Teachers often have to try to figure out if the perpetually quiet student is quiet because that is the norm in his native country, because he doesn't understand English, because he has a delay in speech development, or because he is simply not talkative.

For example, Ms. Wijaksana shared the story of working with a student whose family was from Russia. After multiple unsuccessful parent-teacher conferences, Ms. Wijaksana was asked to attend a meeting. During that time, Ms. Wijaksana observed that every time the teacher mentioned his concerns regarding the student's social behaviors (which was the reason the teacher had requested the meeting), the parents responded, "But she is doing well in school."

After seeing how these exchanges were elevating the frustration levels of those involved, Ms. Wijaksana asked the parent, "How do Russian schools handle behavior issues?" The parent replied, "They don't. That's the parent's job." Thus, the limited cultural understanding on both sides led to a great deal of confusion, which—without a well-established relationship in place— could have eroded the trust between home and school.

PERSPECTIVES ON THE IEP MEETING

Ms. Wijaksana has participated in "countless" IEP meetings with CLD families. The district in which she works includes speakers of more than 50 different languages, and the elementary school where she currently serves has a student population that is predominantly Asian or Middle Eastern. In the past, Ms. Wijaksana has participated in as many as 130 IEP meetings with CLD families in an academic year. In her current position, Ms. Wijaksana estimates that number is closer to 50. Her experiences and her prior training as a clinical psychologist enable her to view an IEP meeting for a CLD student as a group of individuals. She recognizes that everyone is there in the student's best interest, but also that each person has a different perspective on the process. As she puts it, "There are lots of pieces" to think about.

Communication

As a result of her experiences working with CLD families as part of their IEP team, Ms. Wijaksana views the process as primarily an exercise in communication. In her view, who communicates what, and how he or she is communicating it, will determine whether or not the meeting will be successful. She explains, "When there's negativity about anything in a meeting, it's always the result of a miscommunication. Either someone has said the wrong thing or said the right thing the wrong way." As such, ensuring that everyone is "on the same page" is of utmost importance.

Ms. Wijaksana's frustration extends to finding sufficiently trained translators as well. From her point of view, while the IEP team relies heavily on their input, there are often issues of being uncertain about the translator's understanding of what the school is trying to say and how those messages are being related to the families. She has seen members of the IEP team openly question what the translator is saying to the families with statements like, "The rest of us have no idea what you are saying. Are you telling them [the parents] what we said, or are you putting a spin on it?"

Clearly, situations like this are problematic in terms of building and maintaining open lines of communication. Worse still is when the IEP team must rely on a child's sibling to act as translator. When this happens, the problem of whether or not the translator understands the special education process in general and the commonly used acronyms in particular is exacerbated.

A similar issue exists with regard to evaluators. As Ms. Wijaksana points out, a bilingual evaluator is not the same thing as someone who is bilingual and evaluates. In a district of nearly 75,000 students who speak nearly 60 languages, there are only 4 bilingual evaluators, all of whom speak Spanish. Lack of access to trained evaluators (often due to budget constraints) makes it difficult for the IEP team to determine accurately whether the child actually needs special education services.

The result is that IEP teams sometimes must rely on their own inferences and anecdotes as they attempt to create a profile of the student as a learner. These issues regarding communication and language accessibility have arisen with others: the principal (Chapter 1), the general education teacher (Chapter 2), the ESOL teacher (Chapter 4), the translator (Chapter 8), and the guidance counselor (Chapter 12).

Scheduling

Another challenge that Ms. Wijaksana often faces is scheduling. The typical K–12 school is open seven to eight hours a day, usually closing in the early to mid-afternoon. It is not uncommon for the families of CLD students to have work schedules that prevent them from attending meetings during the school day.

For example, Ms. Wijaksana shared the story of one Arabic-speaking student from Morocco whose father worked three jobs—custodian, taxi driver, and package deliverer—and thus was unable to be present at the proposed meeting time. After a few of the members made comments like, "Well, I guess this isn't that important to him," the meeting proceeded without him. Ms. Wijaksana expressed regret that the rigid time constraints of the school day were a barrier to this father's involvement in his child's education: "We say it's consensus, but it plays out like power."

SUGGESTIONS FOR IMPROVEMENT

Throughout our conversations, Ms. Wijaksana reiterated her belief that there are many "pieces" to consider in an IEP meeting for a CLD student. However, when it comes to making suggestions for improvement, Ms. Wijaksana feels that there is only one general, overarching recommendation worth considering—the need for IEP team members to endeavor to recognize the perspectives of other IEP team members.

Strive for Mutual Understanding

Ms. Wijaksana's experiences with CLD families allow for several suggestions for improving the process. When asked about what makes for a successful IEP meeting, Ms. Wijaksana's reply was deceivingly simple: "It all depends." Every aspect of the IEP meeting—its structure, its interactions, and its outcomes—relies on the people who are sitting at the table.

If team members are interested in establishing rapport, then it is likely that they will create effective working relationships. If there is tension, then there will likely be resistance to one another's ideas. In other words, sometimes an IEP meeting will "work," and sometimes it won't. However, the underlying issues regarding trust and communication are often rooted in the school's lack of understanding of other cultures and the families' lack of understanding about American schools (Rossetti, Sauer, Bui, & Ou, 2018).

For example, Ms. Wijaksana commented that teachers are often confused by a parent's reaction to the word "disabled." When used to describe a physical condition such as cerebral palsy, parents seem to embrace the term, but when used with regard to academic performance such as dyslexia, parents are resistant. Ms. Wijaksana's conversations with other professionals lead her to believe that the differing reactions are the result of how the family's native country views disability.

In some cultures, individuals with disabilities are treated as cast-offs or "less-thans." Thus, it is easy to see why parents' reaction to the news that their child has been found eligible for special education services would be negative. As a result, when the "disabled" label is met with a negative reaction, Ms. Wijaksana shared that school personnel often feel "insulted," a feeling that is made worse because the school-based personnel feel that they are "only trying to do the right thing."

Clearly, school personnel would benefit from the opportunity to know more about the cultures of the students with whom they work. As mentioned earlier, Ms. Wijaksana herself completed one course on multiculturalism as part of her degree program. Many states require that teachers take a class in working with students in special education and/or a class in working with English Language Learners, but there are few (if any) that require coursework in working with dually identified students. Some districts address this gap in teachers' knowledge by providing professional development opportunities, but these are becoming more scarce as budgetary belts get tightened.

QUESTIONS FOR DISCUSSION/REFLECTION

- How important is the school psychologist's role in the IEP meetings for CLD students? How does a school psychologist's position shape his or her perspectives on the process?
- Ms. Wijaksana talks about the importance of trusting relationships between families and schools. How can these be formed and maintained? Who is responsible for their formation and maintenance?
- How can schools be "welcoming" in a meaningful way for CLD families?
- What can (should) schools, districts, and teacher education programs do to address the issues raised by Ms. Wijaksana? For example, how can schools re-envision how IEP meetings are scheduled?
- How can a school demonstrate its willingness to work with families? How can families demonstrate their willingness to work with schools?
- When describing the interactions she often sees at IEP meetings with CLD families, Ms. Wijaksana says, "There is what's true, and then there's the truth." What do you think she means by that statement?
- How would you rate your own understanding of other cultures?

ADDITIONAL RESOURCES

These articles, books, reports, and/or websites provide more information about the topics mentioned in this chapter.

Cultural Competence

Larke, P. J. (2013). Cultural Diversity Awareness Inventory: Assessing the sensitivity of preservice teachers. *Action in Teacher Education, 12,* 23–30.

Lynch, E. W., & Hanson, M. J. (Eds.). (1992). *Developing cross-cultural competence: A guide for working with young children and their families*. Baltimore: Paul H. Brookes Publishing.

Macmillan's Cultural Awareness: http://www.macmillanenglish.com/life-skills/cultural-awareness/

Bilingual Evaluation

Boerma, T., & Blom, E. (2017). Assessment of bilingual children: What if testing both languages is not possible? *Journal of Communication Disorders, 66,* 65–76.

Caesar, L. G., & Kohler, P. D. (2007). The state of school-based bilingual assessment: Actual practice versus recommended guidelines. *Language, Speech & Hearing Services in Schools, 38,* 190–200.

Cline, T. (1998). The assessment of special educational needs for bilingual children. *British Journal of Special Education, 25,* 159–164.

Dollaghana, C. A., Horner, E. A, & Oetting, J. (2011). Bilingual language assessment: A meta-analysis of diagnostic accuracy. *Journal of Speech, Language & Hearing Research, 54,* 1077–1088.

O'Byron, C., & Rogers, M. R. (2010). Bilingual school psychologists' assessment practices with English language learners. *Psychology in the Schools, 47,* 1018–1034.

Olvera, P., & Olvera, V. (2015). Bilingual school psychology: Challenges and opportunities. *Contemporary School Psychology, 19,* 165–172.

Rodríguez, A., & Rodríguez, D. (2017). English learners with learning disabilities: What is the current state? *Insights on Learning Disabilities, 14,* 97–112.

Sotelo-Dynega, M. (2015). What is a bilingual school psychologist? A national survey of the credentialing bodies of school psychologists: Implications for the assessment of bilinguals. *Journal of Psychoeducational Assessment, 33,* 247–258.

School Psychologists and IEPs

Arivett, D., Rust, J., Brissie, J., & Dansby, V. (2007). Special education teachers' perceptions of school psychologists in the context of individualized education program meetings. *Education, 127,* 378–388.

Harris, B., Sullivan, A. L., Oades-Sese, G. V., & Sotelo-Dynega, M. (2015). Culturally and linguistically responsive practices in psychoeducational reports for English language learners. *Journal of Applied School Psychology, 31,* 141–166.

Kasky-Hernández, L., & Cates, G. L. (2015). Role of psychologists in interdisciplinary relations in special education. *Advances in Special Education, 30,* 81–94.

Kellems, R. O., Springer, B., Wilkins, M. K., & Anderson, C. (2016). Collaboration in transition assessment: School psychologists and special educators working together to improve outcomes for students with disabilities. *Preventing School Failure, 60,* 215–221.

Lanfranchi, A. (2014). The significance of the interculturally competent school psychologist for achieving equitable education outcomes for migrant students. *School Psychology International, 35,* 544–558.

Sullivan, A. L., & Proctor, S. L. (2016). The shield or the sword? Revisiting the debate on racial disproportionality in special education and implications for school psychologists. *School Psychology Forum, 10,* 278–288.

Vega, D., Lasser, J., & Afifi, A. (2016). School psychologists and the assessment of culturally and linguistically diverse students. *Contemporary School Psychology, 20,* 218–229.

Weddle, S. A., Spencer, T. D., Kajian, M., & Petersen, D. B. (2016). An examination of a multitiered system of language support for culturally and linguistically diverse preschoolers: Implications for early and accurate identification. *School Psychology Review, 45,* 109–132.

Chapter Ten

The Specialist's Voice

"Everyone has to take a turn."

The role of a specialist in an Individualized Education Program (IEP) meeting is to provide data and other input related to student performance in specialized areas, including Speech and Language, Physical Therapy, and/or Occupational Therapy. In addition to providing input on student performance in relation to their direct work with students, specialists provide suggestions for refining goals and measures. Due to their expertise, specialists can shed light on other areas of student performance as it relates to or is caused by communication, sensory skills, motor skills, or other specialized challenges and needs. They also provide suggestions for integrating work toward speech and communication goals into other areas of a child's education and for appropriate instructional modifications (Dalien, 2014; District of Columbia Public Schools, 2011).

For this chapter, we spoke with Ms. Donos, a speech/language pathologist (S/LP). Ms. Donos has held a position as an S/LP at her current elementary school for 18 years and has prior experience at the secondary level. She holds master's degrees in communication disorders and in administration. She has also completed the training for an administrative license necessary for school principals and assistant principals in the hope that she could take her experience and perspectives in special education to a broader school community. Due to the shortage of speech and language professionals, however, she has not successfully attained an administrative position in spite of numerous interviews because she is too much in demand as a speech/language pathologist.

During her more than 20 years of experience, Ms. Donos has participated in hundreds, if not thousands, of IEP meetings. As an experienced specialist, she has also been actively involved in many eligibility determinations. At the time of the interview, she had 11 IEP meetings on her schedule for the coming month. She works with culturally and linguistically diverse (CLD) and non-CLD students and families alike.

PERSPECTIVES ON CULTURAL AND LINGUISTIC DIVERSITY

Overall, Ms. Donos's district population includes more than 15% English for Speakers of Other Languages (ESOL) learners and over 40% CLD students. Thus, she has worked with many CLD students and families over the years; the CLD groups most dominant at her school, she reports, are Middle Eastern or Asian. Perhaps unlike other schools that may have concentrated centers for CLD students, Ms. Donos notes that all ESOL students receive English-language instruction right in her school building.

Referral of CLD Students and Parent Reactions

Even when a child is an English language learner, she says, teachers notice if a child is not making progress and will refer him for special education services. He then goes to Child Study and receives additional accommodations in the classroom. Then, if challenges and learning issues continue, the student will undergo dual language testing (if interpretation is needed). The normal testing protocols apply.

Once the evaluation process is complete, the school shares information with parents and asks whether interpretation will be needed for a meeting to discuss the evaluation results and eligibility. When the eligibility committee meets to determine which, if any, of the 14 eligibility areas the student may fall into, parents are normally supportive and on board with the school recommendations.

While some CLD parents may initially be in denial, when presented with evidence of classroom challenges, they usually realize the need for special education services. In only 10 cases over the course of 18 years at her school have parents refused eligibility, primarily because parents view a label as a stigma. This has usually involved a male student from a Middle Eastern cultural background.

In Ms. Donos's experience, most CLD families are grateful for whatever services the school can offer. This is particularly the case, she believes, with families from lower socioeconomic backgrounds. Generally speaking, they tend to ensure that their children come to school clean and well prepared, do their best to attend meetings, and rarely contest school findings or recommendations.

PERSPECTIVES ON IEP MEETINGS

Ms. Donos believes that her school is unique. At other schools, meetings with CLD parents typically do not go well. Parents do not understand the process and findings because schools do not explain them clearly. As a result, parents cannot be equal partners. Other schools may have had good policies for CLD families, but in reality, they—both the schools and the parents—were overwhelmed.

By contrast, Ms. Donos believes that her school is committed to transparency, open communication with parents, equality, and working as a team to ensure the best outcome for students. Her school also provides extensive links to outside service providers, including low- or no-cost options outside the school system, as well as to resources within it, such as a parent resource center. This contributes to the development of trust, open communication, and a commitment to putting students first.

Trust and Communication

Ms. Donos believes that her school works hard to earn parents' trust and has a sincere commitment to transparency throughout the process. School staff work to ensure that parents know that their children are valued. Every meeting starts with positive yet sincere comments and then proceeds to a neutral discussion of needs based on classroom examples. Ms. Donos believes that by starting with this approach, schools can build a bond with parents and earn their trust.

In every meeting, staff use simple language and a deliberate pace so that parents know that "This is what we're going to do," and "This is what will happen next." Every effort is made to ensure that parents and the school IEP team are in agreement at each step of the process. Furthering this trust, no one wields clout in meetings, and parents are never forced to sign their child's IEP without a full understanding of what it stipulates.

Language and Communication

From the beginning of the process, staff are sensitive to the need for interpretation and translation. "Everyone deserves to understand and to be understood," she says. Students receive dual language assessments as needed, and the school provides translation and interpretation for meetings. As noted above, with or without translators, meeting personnel are very clear and use plain English to explain instructional and procedural areas of concern, and take time to answer questions and provide clears explanations.

School personnel routinely stop a lot, provide numerous examples, and elicit questions. Whenever possible, teachers bring work samples to illustrate some of the areas of challenge prior to discussing goals and possible instructional approaches. This aligns with the emphasis on reducing the "us versus them" dynamic that typifies many meetings, as noted by the principal (Chapter 1), the general education teacher (Chapter 2), the special education teacher (Chapter 3), the ESOL teacher (Chapter 4), the advocate (Chapter 5), the parent (Chapter 7), the translator (Chapter 8), and the guidance counselor (Chapter 12).

Contentious Meetings

Although the school endeavors to keep meetings positive, frustrations on either side can contribute to difficulties. Teachers may be frustrated when there is no support at home, when parents ignore forms that the school sends home, or when students repeatedly come to school ill-prepared or poorly supplied without explanation. Parents may become frustrated because they are seeing no progress and blame the school. Although the school staff is committed to working out solutions within the team framework, sometimes parents appeal to advocates for additional assistance.

In Ms. Donos's opinion, bringing an advocate to an IEP meeting indicates that the trust between school and parents has broken down and that the meeting will be contentious. Unfortunately, Ms. Donos says, this happens when parents disagree with the school's findings or proposals and believe they cannot resolve differences within the team. In Ms. Donos's experience, advocates are inevitably a source of conflict for several reasons.

First, Ms. Donos states, advocates always want more than the law provides. Often, they may insist on specific programs or curricula, whether or not they are appropriate or used by the district. Sometimes they write goals for the school and even write the parent portion of the IEP. This inevitably leads to a dynamic of conflict rather than collaboration. In all her years in IEP meetings, however, Ms. Donos has never known a CLD parent to bring an advocate. Meetings with CLD families are rarely contentious, largely due to school efforts to foster trust.

SUGGESTIONS FOR IMPROVEMENT

In light of her years of experience and her perspectives as both a specialist and someone trained as an administrator, Ms. Donos has numerous insights for improving the special education process, both in terms of IEP meetings and instructional services. Her primary suggestion is that more be done to foster true inclusion.

Train Teachers in Special Education

An issue that arises early in the identification process is the preparation of general education teachers so that they are able to participate in the Child Study process. Ms. Donos believes that teachers should take at least one class in special education so that they are prepared for the identification and evaluation of students and have an understanding of the IEP process itself.

This is a theme that has emerged in other interviews, notably in discussion with the general education teacher (Chapter 2). Ms. Klog, the general education teacher, was seeking training so that she would be empowered to make a more significant contribution to the eligibility process and in subsequent instructional services. She was also specifically interested in learning to collect data on student performance.

Ms. Donos is seeking better training for general education teachers to support her own work, rather than necessarily empowering the general education teachers. She is concerned with their ability to collect useful data, particularly during the evaluation phase of the process. Ms. Donos also believes that it is important that the teachers understand how to collect data because she views their efforts, at present, to be inadequate.

In addition to providing skills and insights that will improve the efficacy of general education teachers who have special education students in their classrooms, Ms. Donos believes that special education teachers are also somewhat deficient in their approaches to data collection. The ability and willingness to collect information systematically on student performance are critical so that teachers can better contribute to IEP meetings and instructional planning.

For example, in Ms. Donos's experience, the area of speech in which ESOL students struggle is articulation. Once they are eligible for special education and begin receiving services, she works sequentially from sounds to phrases to expected sentences, documenting progress in each area. Specialists' instructional time with students, however, represents a relatively small portion of their IEP service hours. For this reason, information on speech performance in other settings would allow her to better address student needs.

Citing a recent example, Ms. Donos was troubled by a recent exchange with a special education teacher. The teacher did not know how to prepare background information in advance of an IEP meeting and thus did not have records in writing to draw from about a student's performance. She reports that the teacher came to her and said, "What should I write?" and needed input from Ms. Donos, who sees the student far less often but keeps far more detailed records and data logs.

As discussed in Chapter 2, training for general education teachers in special education is a known need (e.g., European Agency for Development in Special Needs Education, 2010). Outside of the need to prepare special educators for work with CLD students (as described by Ms. Matalino in Chapter 3) and the need for ongoing inservice work to avoid burnout (mentioned by Ms. Klog in Chapter 2), there is little written about the ongoing professional development needs of special education teachers. Although Dr. Moudry in Chapter 1 specifically mentions the need for training in data collection, this is apparently a weak point in special education teacher preparation programs (Ikkanda, n.d.).

Promote Inclusion through Teaching Teams and Assignments

Ms. Donos's school is organized using an inclusion model with only a single self-contained classroom in the school. She is very positive in describing the school's inclusion model, in which team teaching by both the grade-level classroom teacher and the special education teacher is practiced effectively. In this way, students have the accommodations they need, differentiation of teaching methods, additional assistance, and fewer pullouts.

The teams are usually fairly constant from year to year with the same teachers repeatedly co-teaching with special education teachers. This is because very few teachers are willing to co-teach with a special educator. Ms. Donos adamantly believes, however, that more rotation among the pairs would broaden the school's base of experience and would allow more teachers to differentiate their instruction more effectively, even when they are not co-teaching. Thus, in her opinion, there should be a mandate that "everyone has to take a turn."

There is also a need for more training for collaborative teaching teams in how to maximize their instructional roles to better serve all students in an inclusive classroom, especially since training in this area seems to portend positive results (Sharma, Forlin, & Loreman, 2008). Another promising note is that general education teachers who do collaborate and work in an inclusive classroom have a much more positive view of special education students than their peers without the same experience (Avramidis, Bayliss, & Burden, 2000).

In addition to requiring grade-level general educators to rotate through a special education teaming arrangement, Ms. Donos believes that special educators would benefit from rotating through various grade-level assignments. Teachers become comfortable in their silos, and due to the standards-based nature of evaluation in her school system, they focus narrowly on "checking the boxes" required for their grade level.

Due to this narrow perspective, Ms. Donos believes that teachers sometimes miss the fuller picture of children's needs. As a result, teachers in the upper grades discover issues that could have been addressed sooner. In other words, if teachers rotated through various grade levels, there could be a more consistent approach and understanding of the demands on a student over the course of his elementary school years.

QUESTIONS FOR DISCUSSION/REFLECTION

- How important is a specialist's role in the IEP meetings for CLD students? How does a specialist's position shape his or her perspectives on the process?
- Ms. Donos remarks that all teachers should "take a turn" at co-teaching. Is it productive to force teachers into team-teaching arrangements? What kinds of measures could facilitate these partnerships or incentivize teachers?
- Should all teachers receive training in special education? Why or why not?
- Ms. Donos believes that her school is unique in terms of its effectiveness in working with CLD students and families. What aspects of your school or classroom contribute to effectiveness with this population? What aspects detract?
- Do you think that data collection presents an undue burden and distraction from instructional time? Are there ways in which this can be facilitated?
- How can barriers to collaboration be overcome?
- What other specialized positions play a role in an IEP meeting for a CLD student?

ADDITIONAL RESOURCES

These articles, books, reports, and/or websites provide more information about the topics mentioned in this chapter.

Training General Education Teachers in Special Education

American Association of Colleges of Teacher Education. (2014). *Preparing general education teachers to improve outcomes for students with disabilities.* Retrieved from https://www.ncld.org/wp-content/uploads/2014/11/aacte_ncld_recommendation.pdf

Coady, M. R., Harper, C., & de Jong, E. J. (2015). Aiming for equity: Preparing mainstream teachers for inclusion or inclusive classrooms? *TESOL Quarterly, 50,* 340–368. http://doi.org/10.1002/tesq.223

Navarro, S. B., Panagiotis, Z., Gesa, R. F., & Sampson, D. G. (2016). Developing teachers' competences for designing inclusive learning experiences. *Journal of Educational Technology & Society, 19,* 17–27.

Shaffer, L., & Thomas-Brown, K. (2015). Enhancing teacher competency through co-teaching and embedded professional development. *Journal of Education and Training Studies, 3*(3). https://doi.org/10.11114/jets.v3i3.685

Training for Special Education Teachers

Katkin, T., & Murphy, J. (2017). *Why special education teachers need more training.* Retrieved from https://www.teacherswithapps.com/why-special-education-teachers-need-more-training/

Wakeman, S. (n.d.) *Data collection: An introduction.* Modules Addressing Special Education and Teaching. Retrieved from http://mast.ecu.edu/modules/dc_intro/concept/

Webster, J. (2017). Data collection for special education. ThoughtCo.com, June 8. Retrieved from https://www.thoughtco.com/data-collection-for-special-education-3110861

Teaching Teams and Assignments

Cook, L., & Friend, M. (2010). The state of the art of collaboration on behalf of students with disabilities. *Journal of Educational and Psychological Consultation, 20*(1), 1–8. https://doi.org/10.1080/10474410903535398

Embury, D. C., & Clarke, L. (2017). *How training of special education teachers has changed to prepare them for inclusion.* Retrieved from http://www.friendshipcircle.org/blog/2017/05/11/how-special-education-teachers-are-educated-for-inclusion/

Singh, D. K. (2006). *Preparing general education teachers for inclusion.* ERIC ED 499-13. https://files.eric.ed.gov/fulltext/ED499013.pdf

Chapter Eleven

The Transition Services Specialist's Voice

"The buck stops here."

The primary role of the transition services specialist in an Individualized Education Program (IEP) meeting is to provide information to students' families about options and eligibility criteria for appropriate community or adult services once the student leaves high school. In addition, the transition services specialist supports and assists the student[1] in identifying community or adult services that may assist him or her in achieving post-graduation goals. In essence, the transition services specialist acts as a "bridge" between the world of school and the world of gainful employment, vocational training, or higher education.

The transition services specialist we interviewed, Dr. Bulumko, has been working in his school system for nearly 30 years. He started his career as an English teacher at the secondary level. His experiences working with students with special needs led him to pursue both a master's and a doctoral degree in special education. For the past 15 years, Dr. Bulumko has worked primarily as a transition services specialist, but he also teaches classes as an adjunct professor for several local universities.

PERSPECTIVES ON CULTURAL AND LINGUISTIC DIVERSITY

Dr. Bulumko's position as a transition services specialist provides him with several unique perspectives on working with culturally and linguistically diverse (CLD) students. First and foremost, he speaks a great deal about the dichotomy of expectations versus reality. Dr. Bulumko notes that all parents—regardless of their background—"struggle" with adult services. While they may have become inured to the "ins and outs" of special education during their child's K–12 years, the postsecondary world is an unfamiliar place that can be overwhelming and confusing. Further, many parents are in denial about their child's abilities. In his experience, this is even more true for CLD families.

Expectations versus Reality

According to Dr. Bulumko, CLD parents' refusal to accept their child's limitations is due to several factors (such as language barriers) and is often accompanied by their "ludicrous" dreams for the child's future. For example, Dr. Bulumko shared the story of a young man who was nonverbal, had "severe" cognitive delays, and whose family spoke Japanese at home. Despite being told for several years that their son's options in terms of further academic opportunities might be limited, his parents insisted on exploring options for applying to a four-year college.

In situations like these, Dr. Bulumko shared that he is often put in the awkward position of having to bring CLD parents "down to earth" in terms of what is realistic and what is not, and they are often unresponsive to what he has to say. As a result, Dr. Bulumko often calls on other school-based personnel to support his viewpoint, noting that sometimes, "It takes a village to crush a dream."

PERSPECTIVES ON THE IEP MEETING

Dr. Bulumko has noticed three general "themes" in terms of working with CLD families over the course of his career as a transition services specialist—denial, different outcomes, and quality of communication. In Dr. Bulumko's experience, each of these plays an important role when working with CLD families in IEP meetings.

Denial

Dr. Bulumko reports that CLD parents often wait until the end of their student's school year before acting upon recommendations made by the IEP team during the previous months or, in some cases, years. While it is not uncommon for parents to be in denial about their child's diagnosis, Dr. Bulumko believes that CLD families' delays in following up on transition-related suggestions from the IEP team are further exacerbated by parents' lack of understanding about the diagnosis.

Although their child may have been receiving special education services since elementary or middle school, CLD parents are often still uncertain about the label their child received at the end of high school. Dr. Bulumko attributes this to CLD parents' hesitance to question the school-based IEP team members, whom the families see as figures of authority.

As Dr. Bulumko puts it, parents do not see themselves as "on the same level" as the school-based IEP team members and therefore do not feel as though their input is worthwhile. This echoes in some ways the "us versus them" dynamic that has been discussed by the principal (Chapter 1), the general education teacher (Chapter 2), the special education teacher (Chapter 3), the English for Speakers of Other Languages (ESOL) teacher (Chapter 4), the advocate (Chapter 5), the parent (Chapter 7), the translator (Chapter 8), and the guidance counselor (Chapter 12).

Different Outcomes

It is Dr. Bulumko's experience that parents who are native English speakers are often much more active in IEP meetings than are CLD parents. For example, the former ask questions and make suggestions. On the other hand, CLD parents' perceptions that the other IEP team members are the ones who are "in charge" means that questions often go unasked and suggestions go unmade. As a result, teachers' goals for students are not—in Dr. Bulumko's words—"status-blind."

In other words, students from non-CLD families often are presented with more—and more varied—postsecondary opportunities than are students from CLD families. Thus, a student's language or background determines the quality of services or referrals suggested by the IEP team members in general and the transition services specialist in particular.

Quality of Communication

A third way in which IEP meetings for CLD students differ from those who are non-CLD pertains to the quality of communication between the school-based IEP team members and the families. Dr. Bulumko cautioned that team members should "watch what they say and how they say it." This can be interpreted in two different ways.

For non-CLD families, Dr. Bulumko says that it is important to be mindful of what is being said because there is a tendency for these parents to be quick to point out an error or to seize an opportunity to request further clarification or information. For CLD families, the admonition to watch one's words means something different. Dr. Bulumko reports that school-based IEP team members often wonder if parents understand what transition means or what the referrals have to do with the student's future. In these situations, Dr. Bulumko believes that IEP team members need to be sure that the language and terminology used are understood by the families.

SUGGESTIONS FOR IMPROVEMENT

In addition to discussing the importance of making sure that all IEP team members are "on the same page," particularly in terms of language and terminology, Dr. Bulumko also makes several suggestions to make an IEP team meeting more effective overall. These include having realistic goals, allowing for more supports, and highlighting the value of transition services.

Manage the Expectations

When asked about what changes could make a CLD student's IEP meeting run more smoothly, particularly in regard to students' prospects for postsecondary opportunities, Dr. Bulumko opined that IEP team members should attempt to lower their expectations. As mentioned earlier in this chapter, Dr. Bulumko feels that many CLD parents have "ludicrous" goals for their child. By having more realistic expectations, Dr. Bulumko feels that there would be less frustration and anger at IEP meetings.

However, Dr. Bulumko feels that the fault of holding overly high expectations rests not only with parents, but with the child's elementary and middle school teachers as well. His advice to them? "Don't promise too much. That way, they [the parents] won't ask for unrealistic things like too many accommodations when they meet me." Given that there is a need for teachers at the secondary level to know more about how to work with CLD students receiving special education services (Trainor, Murray, & Kim, 2016), it seems reasonable for Dr. Bulumko to suggest that elementary and middle school teachers undergo the same preparation.

Provide More Resources

Dr. Bulumko has noticed that parents often do not act on the recommendations he makes. He wonders why this is. Is it about the parents' immigration status? Are they wary of relying on the school or the government for assistance? Something else? Since he cannot get the answers from the parents themselves, Dr. Bulumko feels that providing additional resources such as tutorial, translation, or transportation services to help parents follow up on the IEP team's suggestions would prove helpful for everyone.

Elevate the Importance of Transition Services

In addition to providing additional resources for parents, Dr. Bulumko also suggests that the importance of transition services be made more clear to all IEP team members. In his opinion, reducing caseloads is one way to do this.

Since he began working as a transition services specialist, Dr. Bulumko has seen the number of students for whom he is responsible increase from 15 per year to over 70. In order to work with all of them over the course of an academic year, Dr. Bulumko is unable to spend a meaningful amount of time with each individual student. As a result, both students and families don't fully understand his role or its importance. This is especially problematic given the relatively low percentages of postsecondary students with disabilities actively engaged in their communities as employees of local businesses or as students at postsecondary institutions (Mazzotti & Rowe, 2015).

Parents' misunderstanding of transition services is intensified when a transition services specialist is allotted only one IEP meeting lasting one to two hours in which to share his thoughts. Instead, Dr. Bulumko believes that the transition services specialist should be allowed to meet with parents and students for longer periods of time and more frequently than is currently typical. As he puts it, "What I have to say is more than can be expressed in a 'one and done' approach."

QUESTIONS FOR DISCUSSION/REFLECTION

- How important is the transition specialist's role in the IEP meetings for CLD students? How does a transition services specialist's position shape his or her perspectives on the process?
- Dr. Bulumko's statement, "It takes a village to crush a dream" might evoke strong feelings. What are your thoughts on this? To what extent is it true or untrue in your experience?
- Dr. Bulumko thinks that transition services should be discussed in a separate meeting. What do you see as the pros and the cons of this approach?
- What steps might schools take to help ensure that parents and families understand the importance of transition services?
- What transition services are available for students in your school or district?
- Is saying "Don't promise too much" helpful advice for IEP teams who are working with CLD families? Why or why not?
- What steps might schools or districts take to ensure that their vocational goals are status-blind?

NOTE

1. Students receiving special education services are expected to be present at (or to provide input for) their IEP meetings starting at age 14.

ADDITIONAL RESOURCES

These articles, books, reports, and/or websites provide more information about the topics mentioned in this chapter.

Transition Specialists

Hamblet, E. C. (2014). Nine strategies to improve college transition planning for students with disabilities. *Teaching Exceptional Children, 46,* 53–59. https://doi.org/10.1177/004005991404600306

Mazzotti, V. L., Test, D. W., & Mustian, A. L. (2012). Secondary transition evidence-based practices and predictors: Implications for policymakers. *Journal of Disability Policy Studies, 25,* 5–18. https://doi.org/10.1177/1044207312460888

Piotner, A. J., Mazzotti, V. L., Rose, C. A., & Carlson-Britting, K. B. (2015). Factors associated with enhanced knowledge and use of secondary transition evidence-based practices. *Teacher Education and Special Education, 39,* 28–46. https://doi.org/10.1177/0888406415599430

Supporting CLD Families

Ellis A. L., Grillo L. M., & Durham J. (2017). Personnel preparation in transition education. In A. L. Ellis (Ed.), *Transitioning children with disabilities: Studies in inclusive education* (pp. 27–42). Rotterdam: Sense Publishers.

Greene, G. (2011). *Transition planning for culturally and linguistically diverse youth.* Baltimore, MD: Brookes Publishing Company.

Ju, S., Zhang, D., & Landmar, L. J. (2018). Culturally and linguistically diverse family involvement in transition planning: A research synthesis. *Journal of Special Education Leadership, 31,* 16–26.

Povenmire-Kirk, T. C., Bethune, L. K., Alverson, C. Y., & Kahn, L. G. (2015). A journey, not a destination: Developing cultural competence in secondary transition. *Teaching Exceptional Children, 47,* 319–328. https://doi.org/10.1177/0040059915587679

Chapter Twelve

The Guidance Counselor's Voice

"I take the back door."

Since the enactment of Individuals with Disabilities Education Act (IDEA), guidance counselors have taken a more active role in Individualized Education Program (IEP) meetings. When present, the guidance counselor collaborates with the other school-based IEP team members to make recommendations, to provide their expertise in child development, and to ensure that the student receives the services agreed upon by the team. More and more often, guidance counselors are also being called on to conduct assessments of students in advance of IEP meetings.

Ms. Cialmhar is a guidance counselor who divides her time between a middle school and a high school in a district with a significant population of culturally and linguistically diverse (CLD) students. One-half of her middle school's student population is Latino, as is one-third of the high school students. Her position is specifically to serve as the counselor for students enrolled in ESOL in each school. She has 17 years of experience as a guidance counselor in her district and 9 in another district.

Ms. Cialmhar started her career as a teacher in a third district, during which time she transitioned from teaching to counseling. She undertook that transition as the outgrowth of extensive work with parent groups in the evenings, which helped her to realize the larger needs of the immigrant community in U.S. schools. Along the way, she also became certified as an interpreter.

Ms. Cialmhar has participated in many IEP meetings over the years and considers herself a strong advocate for parents and students. She also engages in numerous professional activities outside the school, including a state coalition for immigrant families, and work with refugee groups, immigrant leadership councils, and legal aid groups working on behalf of immigrants. She is also actively working with undocumented students who are at risk.

When we interviewed Ms. Cialmhar, she had just returned from a conference on working with dually identified students, those receiving both English for Speakers of Other Languages (ESOL) and special education instruction. According to Ms. Cialmhar, even in her district, which has provided ESL instruction to a significant immigrant community since the 1970s, very few teachers are prepared to work with this population.

For example, many teachers frequently use the term "dualie" when referring to CLD students who receive special education services. Ms. Cialmhar avidly dislikes this term because she believes it stigmatizes the students. Instead, she prefers to advocate for students and parents in this group and to empower them by teaching them about their rights. She has supported local advocacy groups with formal training for parents on the educational system, their rights, and even advocacy practices.

PERSPECTIVES ON CULTURAL AND LINGUISTIC DIVERSITY

Based on her many years of work with the CLD student and parent population, as well as being a bilingual professional representative of this group herself, Ms. Cialmhar offers extensive inside perspectives on experiences she has encountered in various schools. Specifically, numerous factors shape the school experiences of immigrant students, particularly those from difficult situations in their home countries. These factors may be invisible to schools, but have a significant mark on students.

Background Experiences

Many students emigrating from countries characterized by war, dislocation, or violence arrive in U.S. schools in various states of trauma or post-traumatic stress. Some have gone through a harrowing process to immigrate, including voyaging north with "coyotes," being arrested and detained, and/or living in shelters without a parent or guardian while sponsors are identified.

Many of these students, once they are settled, attend school all day and then work until late at night. In some cases, they are sending money back to families in Central America who need to pay protection from gangs. Ms. Cialmhar believes that schools do not understand this and see a student's failure to participate in school life and to achieve academically as the result of poor effort or attitude.

Cultural Issues

There are larger factors that shape the educational experiences of even those CLD students who have experienced a less stressful immigration process. Numerous factors shape their ability to succeed. First, there is the process of shifting cultural identity. If students find a welcoming school and community culture that takes an "additive view" of biculturalism and bilingualism, students are much more likely to accept the acculturation process, as it does not entail rejecting their own culture of origin.

This is an invisible but significant issue that is well documented in educational and anthropological research. When schools take a "deficit" view, viewing a student's home culture and first language as barriers to his success in school, the student in turn is more likely to reject the norms of the new culture (e.g., Lima, 2000). Even under ideal circumstances, acquisition of cognitive academic language proficiency (CALP) —the advanced level of language mastery needed for success in secondary school—takes five to seven years (e.g., Collier, 1995). In Ms. Cialmhar's view, acculturation takes about the same amount of time.

Academic Issues

Due to the academic structure and requirements in Ms. Cialmhar's district, students receive no credit toward graduation for ESOL coursework. Thus, they may spend several years in high school with no official progress toward graduation. Although it takes five to seven years to achieve CALP, ESOL programs rarely last that long. This is both good news and bad news. On one hand, students can embark on credit-generating coursework within a few years. On the other, they are undertaking that coursework without sufficient English-language skills to do well in their courses. This in turn puts them at risk for failing the standardized tests required for graduation in core subject areas. The general education coursework is quite challenging.

In order to offset some of these risks, Ms. Cialmhar goes out of her way to work with ESOL teachers and to the extent that they are receptive—general education teachers. She focuses her efforts on several areas. First, she works to build cultural understanding of her students, so that teachers grasp the numerous issues in the lives of many students, particularly those impacting cultural transitions. Next, she provides support so that students may have access to a greater number of academic opportunities.

For example, CLD students are generally underrepresented in advanced or gifted programs. As a result, they are often not included in special summer programs or field trips. Recently, with the support of ESOL teachers, Ms. Cialmhar successfully established three open scholarships for college summer programs designed for high school students at local universities.

Put simply, Ms. Cialmhar works intensively with her student population
so that they have a sense that someone believes in them and that they can set
high expectations for themselves, rather than giving up. For those who are in
ESOL programs and have special education needs, she works hard to promote self-acceptance and developing goals so that students understand that
special education is not a curse, and that they should not fail to set or aban-
don their goals.

PERSPECTIVES ON THE IEP MEETING

IEP meetings can be fraught with pitfalls, with stakeholders coming to the
table with very different sets of expectations and affective stances. Ms.
Cialmhar framed these primarily in terms of the school's and the parents'
perspectives. She sees great contrast between the two.

The School: Great at Following the Process

Although Ms. Cialmhar describes schools as "great at following the special
education process," she also sees a number of discordant dynamics that influence IEP meetings and even create paradoxes in some cases. There are also
numerous dynamics that negatively affect the outcomes in services for students.

First, Ms. Cialmhar notes that, overall, the people at the IEP table are not
there to empower parents. Rather, they are there to serve the system. Often
meetings are rushed because schools do not schedule enough time. Parents
then feel pressured to sign even when they do not understand. This aligns
closely with others who have discussed the "us versus them" dynamic, including the principal (Chapter 1), the general education teacher (Chapter 2),
the special education teacher (Chapter 3), the ESOL teacher (Chapter 4), the
advocate (Chapter 5), the parent (Chapter 7), and the translator (Chapter 8).

Next, there is also a difficult dynamic between special education and
ESOL services and very little dialogue across departments or among teachers. In some cases, this results in a student receiving a label of learning
disabled (LD) merely because he or she cannot access the content in English
or has a speech disability due to second-language acquisition issues.

Furthermore, due to some of the cultural transition issues described
above, sometimes a student who is restless or unfocused for reasons related
to his background experiences may be categorized as LD. In fact, while the
school has the tendency to deny eligibility for services in some cases, para-
doxically there is a district-wide problem with overidentification of CLD
students in the LD category.

In addition to the dynamic between ESOL and special education teachers,
Ms. Cialmhar reports that there is "turfism" among specialists, resulting in a

series of specialists' statements rather than an overall picture of student needs. While teachers often mean well, administrators vary in their ability to keep a meeting focused on a student's best interests. Often, during meetings, there seem to be low expectations for a student, expectations that Ms. Cialmhar says are not the same for white or non-CLD students.

Translation and Interpretation

As the principal (Chapter 1), the general education teacher (Chapter 2), the ESOL teacher (Chapter 4), and the translator (Chapter 8) have discussed, a significant issue in IEP meetings is that of translation and interpretation. It is not legally required that the IEP itself be translated, and even if draft goals go home prior to the meeting, they go in English. Thus, although meetings must have interpreters for parents who request them, parents often arrive at the meeting unprepared for what will be discussed.

In terms of the impact of an interpreter, it varies. Generally, Ms. Cialmhar believes that her district does not have enough qualified interpreters. Some are not certified as interpreters, while others do not have a background in special education. This creates problems in communication because those who are not trained then translate inappropriately.

For example, an untrained interpreter or one who is not knowledgeable about special education may translate "cognitive challenges" to communicate that a child "can't think well." Moreover, even knowledgeable interpreters cannot advocate or interfere in the IEP process. While some may try to send subtle messages to parents, it is not their role to explain or otherwise intervene. Due to these barriers, and because of her work in special education and her certification as an interpreter, Ms. Cialmhar has taken it upon herself to provide training for interpreters who will participate in IEP meetings.

Families

Ms. Cialmhar reports that most of the parents that she works with do not have the educational background to read and understand IEPs or other special education–related documents. Most parents do not know their rights and so "are happy with whatever they get."

In addition, some CLD parents reject any special education needs, believing a label carries with it an undesirable stigma. For example, one family rejected the use of a hearing aid to help a hearing-impaired child. Many CLD parents also deny emotional issues. Except for those who have participated in parent workshops, parents are usually silent in IEP meetings. As a result, sometimes services are not provided, even if there is documentation to support them.

When CLD students attend, most are equally uninformed of their rights. For example, Ms. Cialmhar reports that there are sometimes intrusions on students' privacy. In one case, a student was asked if he had documents to live in the United States. In another, a student was told to stop working to improve his school performance. Neither student realized that he was not required to respond to these questions or comments.

Ms. Cialmhar has numerous ways in which she tries to help. First, she can identify quickly when students are not making progress and begin to stagnate in ESOL. In many cases, teachers believe that "it's the language," so the students are not referred for a special education evaluation.

It is very difficult to get students into the screening process unless they come with documentation of a disability from their home country. In order to ensure that students are evaluated, Ms. Cialmhar often takes what she calls "the back door," telling parents to write a note saying that their child is not learning. Once parents do this, the school has 60 days to respond and initiate evaluation.

Another way that Ms. Cialmhar tries to support CLD parents and improve outcomes for students is connecting parents in order to develop an informal support group. She mentors these parent groups so that they can begin to understand the special education process and become better advocates for their children. She also conducts parent leadership training on various topics for her district's Hispanic Association; she is an unpaid consultant to that group, as well as to similar groups in other jurisdictions.

In addition, her school just approved a parent group coffee hour in the mornings, an *hora de café* that she considers a major breakthrough. She also assists individual parents. If she thinks she can help by advocating for a parent or student in an IEP, she tells the parents that they have the right to bring whomever they want to an IEP meeting so that she can attend.

Unfortunately, in Ms. Cialmhar's experience, the school generally does not like it when parents are empowered. If a parent is "difficult," that is, knows how to advocate for his or her child, there is often a "pre-meeting meeting" during which the school-based members of the IEP team decide what the school's position will be on providing services. Further, Ms. Cialmhar firmly believes that schools respond more quickly to non-CLD parents because the school believes that they know the system and have the resources to navigate it. This, she states adamantly, is discrimination.

SUGGESTIONS FOR IMPROVEMENT

In order to improve the process and ensure equity for all students, Ms. Cialmhar has numerous suggestions. These correspond very closely to the areas described above—improving cultural competence, reducing discrimination, empowering parents, and ensuring clear communication with families—and also align with issues raised in other research with CLD families engaged with the IEP process.

Increase Cultural Competence

School culture is difficult to define, and yet it is something that most people who work in a school can describe. Generally, school culture reflects a set of shared values or beliefs that affect teachers, students, and other staff. This is a subject addressed in numerous books and articles aimed primarily at school principals. The core principles of a positive school culture boil down to respect among teachers and students, transparency in decision making, support for collaboration, and expectations for ongoing learning for staff and students alike.

As opposed to some principals who just give orders, Ms. Cialmhar describes the principal of the high school where she works as "wonderful" and supportive of sometimes marginalized groups of students that fall into her population. For example, when temporary protected status (a federally determined immigration status) was cut for some national groups in 2017, her principal sent out a video to school personnel about welcoming immigrants and describing how they enrich the communities in which they live.

Nevertheless, there are significant areas for improvement. Ms. Cialmhar notes the importance of cultural respect and competence because teachers provide a mirror for students. If teachers reject their cultures, students feel alienated or ashamed. According to Ms. Cialmhar, this happens all too frequently. For example, Ms. Cialmhar learned recently that one teacher in the school is afraid of her ESOL students, believing that they all belong to gangs. In general, she believes that teachers hold low expectations for CLD students and that discrimination is all too common. She believes that few in the school try to understand what it means to be an immigrant and that schools must listen to students and be open and try to understand.

More darkly, Ms. Cialmhar sees racism in some school or district officials in a position of power. This can be directed at parents, teachers, or other staff who advocate for parents from CLD groups. She has experienced many instances of discrimination within the school. For example, someone recently asked her why, since she is Mexican, she is not in California or New Mexico. Teachers often question or dismiss her viewpoint or suggestions, which she finds offensive because she holds numerous degrees and certifications.

Another example of racism that Ms. Cialmhar has witnessed is CLD parents often marginalized at school events. For example, at a recent school event, the Latino parents were asked to bring food and to clean up after the event. Later, a white woman on the support staff apologized for this. Ms.

Cialmhar does not know how to change this except for educating the school community that CLD parents must be treated as equals.

Culture and belief systems are incredibly difficult to change, which makes fostering cultural competence among teachers and other school staff critical. Assuming a commitment by leadership and school personnel, there are a number of tools and diagnostics available to begin the undertaking (i.e., National Education Association, 2000), which could be a positive means of professional development and empowerment for teachers (Villegas & Lucas, 2002; Vilson, 2015). In addition, in this era of accountability, setting high expectations for students is one of the most important elements for academic achievement, and raising levels of achievement will benefit the school overall.

Communicate More Effectively

Ms. Cialmhar summarizes her views on the need for improved communication as, "School officials need to come down from the clouds and explain how they can help." She is frustrated that, so often, the parents of her CLD students have little idea what is happening in IEP meetings—the services offered, the educational impact, their rights as parents. This applies to lines of communication between school and home, advance communication with parents prior to meetings, the use of simple language rather than jargon in meetings, and the provision of skilled interpretation during meetings.

In terms of communication between school and home, the initiation of parent coffees is a positive step to bring parents into the school. A necessary next step would be more regular communication between teachers and parents, such as those described by Ms. Klog, the general education teacher, and Ms. Hekima, the ESOL teacher. Both described explicit teacher efforts to accommodate parent schedules, establish a relationship prior to any formal meetings or school issues, and communicate openly about students' challenges and needs. All this should come well in advance of IEP meetings.

Ms. Cialmhar focuses intensively on the issue of language barriers and has a simple recommendation to improve the process for families: "Schools should respect Title IV," which requires translation of documents and provision of interpretation services.[1] It does not, however, mandate translation of IEP documents themselves, or require that other written language related to IEP goals and objectives be provided in a family's first language, although some U.S. Department of Education regulatory language suggests that in some cases, it might be beneficial to do (Arizona Ombudsman, 2016).

As reflected in our interviews, current practices of many school districts seem to adhere to the letter of the law—the requirement to provide interpretation for IEP meetings—without going further to ensure that parents understand the purpose of the meeting or the context of the educational goal setting and accommodations. Thus, even when good interpretation is provided at meetings, CLD parents have had no advance communication (or at least none in their native language) regarding the goals of the IEP or even, in some cases, the purpose of the meeting.

Ms. Cialmhar has described in detail how translation and interpretation fall short of CLD families' needs if they are to be equal partners in the IEP process. It seems that a significant improvement would be to ensure that interpreters are certified, rather than merely enlist the services of a bilingual individual in the building.

As others have noted—see Chapters 1, 4, and 8—if interpreters are not trained in special education language and process, they will not be able to adequately convey to parents the true meaning of what is being discussed. While some states have guidelines that require this type of training, the one in which Ms. Cialmhar works is not one of them.

Empower Parents

Ms. Cialmhar has undertaken extensive efforts to develop parent support groups and to work with local community groups to educate parents on school processes and their rights. While there is extensive information in the public domain regarding parent rights in the IEP process, many CLD parents simply do not approach schools with this paradigm in mind. Extensive research has examined this phenomenon, and numerous interviews have proven consistent with those broader findings (e.g., Higgins, 2016; Montelungo, 2014; Zamora, 2015).

There are many tools and guides available for those who want to engage in parent education and advocacy (see "Additional Resources" below). The question of whether they will be used is one of will. If schools understand that investing resources in parent education can result in significantly higher achievement among students, it seems clear that such efforts are worthwhile (U.S. Department of Education, 2014). If not for the sake of equity and social justice, doing so would result in improved CLD student performance. In this era of accountability, that should matter to school leaders.

QUESTIONS FOR DISCUSSION/REFLECTION

- How important is the guidance counselor's role in the IEP meetings for CLD students? How does a guidance counselor's position shape his or her perspectives on the process?
- Ms. Cialmhar comments on the importance of a school's culture. How would you describe the culture in your current school? (If you are not currently working in a school, think about the school you most recently attended.)

- How can schools support respect for all students? Are there subtle barriers reflecting linguistic, cultural, gender, or ethnic differences?
- How should school leaders communicate their expectations for teachers and students?
- Ms. Cialmhar considers herself both a guidance counselor and an activist. What are the benefits of this outlook? The challenges?
- What measures have you taken to further develop your cross-cultural skills and knowledge? How have your cultural skills impacted your career and your ability to be successful in interactions with individuals from other backgrounds?
- Ms. Cialmhar believes in the importance of IEP team members being equal partners. Is that a reasonable or achievable standard? Why or why not?

NOTE

1. As noted in Chapter 8, Title IV specifically stipulates that schools must ensure that parents understand the IEP meeting proceedings, and that procedural safeguards and prior written notice must be written in understandable language and provided in the native language unless it is not feasible to do so (U.S. Department of Education, 2016; Minnesota Department of Education, 2005, pp. 117–118).

ADDITIONAL RESOURCES

These articles, books, reports, and/or websites provide more information about the topics mentioned in this chapter.

School Culture and Cultural Competence

Carrington, S. (1999). Inclusion needs a different school culture. *International Journal of Inclusive Education, 3*(3). https://doi.org/10.1080/136031199285039
Howard, G. R. (2016). *We can't teach what we don't know: White teachers, multiracial schools.* New York: Teachers College Press.
Nelson, S. W., & Guerra, P. L. (2013). Educator beliefs and cultural knowledge: Implications for school improvement efforts. *Educational Administration Quarterly, 50,* 67–95. https://doi.org/10.1177/0013161X13488595
Refugee children in U.S. schools: A toolkit for teachers and school personnel. (n.d.) Retrieved from http://www.brycs.org/documents/upload/Interpretation-Translation-FAQ.pdf
Tolerance.org. (2017). Immigrant and refugee children: A guide for educators and school support staff. *Teaching Tolerance, 55* (Spring). https://www.tolerance.org/magazine/spring-2017/immigrant-and-refugee-children-a-guide-for-educators-and-school-support-staff

Communication and Language

Adult Learning Resource Center. (2003). Involving immigrant and refugee families in their children's schools: Barriers, challenges, and successful strategies. Retrieved from http://www.brycs.org/clearinghouse/clearinghouse-resource.cfm?docnum=1209

Arizona Department of Education. (2018). Does a child's IEP have to be translated into the parents' native language? Retrieved from http://www.azed.gov/disputeresolution/2016/06/23/iep/

Michigan State University, College of Education, Office of K–12 Outreach. (2015). Another IEP: Implementing engagement with parents. Retrieved from http://www.msuk12connect.org/articles/achievement-gaps/special-ed/140-focused-leadership-assuring-learning-for-students-with-ieps-2

U.S. Department of Education. (n.d.). *Establishing partnerships with families.* Retrieved from https://www2.ed.gov/about/offices/list/oela/newcomers-toolkit/chap5.pdf

Empowering Parents

Center for Parent Information and Resources. (2016). *Tools that empower Spanish-speaking parents.* Retrieved from http://www.parentcenterhub.org/tools-for-spanish-speaking-parents/

Lo, L. (2012). Demystifying the IEP process for diverse parents of children with disabilities. *Teaching Exceptional Children,* 14–20. Retrieved from http://olms.cte.jhu.edu/olms2/data/ck/sites/271/files/Week03_Lo.pdf

Poza, L., Brooks, D. B., & Valdes, G. (2014). *Entre familia*: Immigrant parents' strategies for involvement in children's schooling. *School Community Journal, 24*(1), 119–148.

Rogante, F. (2017). *Empowering and equipping Hispanic immigrant parents to actively engage in their children's education.* Hamline University School of Education. Retrieved from https://digitalcommons.hamline.edu/hse_cp/121/

Ruiz, M. I. (2012). Factors that influence the participation of immigrant Latino parents in the special education process of their children with disabilities. Unpublished dissertation, University of New Orleans. Retrieved from http://scholarworks.uno.edu/td/1551

Conclusion

In the preceding chapters, we have heard the voices of different stakeholders who participate in Individualized Education Program (IEP) meetings for culturally and linguistically diverse (CLD) students. In this chapter, we first revisit our approach and our process. Next, we present a summary of findings, based on individual and overlapping issues and recommendations. From these findings, we extend additional recommendations that will improve the IEP process for CLD families and all the stakeholders in the special education process that affects their students.

REVISITING OUR CONCEPTUAL FRAMEWORK

Our approach started with the areas of focus that emerge from research with CLD families involved in special education for their children, most notably that of Blue-Banning, Summers, Frankland, Nelson, and Beegle (2004). There were numerous thematic connections that loosely relate to communication, commitment, equality, skills, trust, and respect. The framework used by Blue-Banning et al. (2004) is useful, and many of the discussions reflected ideas and recommendations similar to research with CLD parents, as we present here.

Communication

This emerged as a dominant theme across the majority of participants. The translator and several others focused on the language used in meetings, and nearly all of the stakeholders we interviewed stressed the importance of being clear, open, and honest. Further, the disability rights attorney also highlighted the importance of using tact (i.e., "deskside manner") when delivering information that might be perceived as negative.

Commitment

While the importance of team members' devotion and loyalty to students was mentioned by several stakeholders, their views on the topic varied widely. The educational advocate remarked that love should have nothing to do with a teacher's ability to do his or her job. In contrast, the general education teacher described in detail her passion for her students and her concerns for their welfare both inside and outside the classroom.

Equality

All of the people we interviewed mentioned equality during their conversations with us. However, the viewpoints shared did not reflect that all IEP team members were on an equal footing in terms of their ability to influence outcomes. In fact, the opposite was true. For example, the guidance counselor and parent both talked at length about how school culture disenfranchises CLD students and families. Some of the stakeholders we interviewed also felt that they were not considered as equals in the process, whether due to their advocacy for students, their own racial or ethnic background, or their professional field.

Skills

Many of the stakeholders with whom we spoke talked about teachers' ability to demonstrate a thorough understanding of best practices. In general, the tone of the comments indicated an overall lack of faith in service providers' ability to fulfill their roles effectively. For example, the principal focused on the need for teachers to be trained in how to collect and interpret data, and the special education teacher spoke of the need for training in cultural and linguistic diversity.

Trust

Stakeholders often mentioned trust as a key aspect of a successful IEP meeting. Unfortunately, while its importance was recognized, it was more common for trust to be mentioned as lacking rather than as present. As an example, both the specialist and transition specialist referred to specific incidents in which it was clear that IEP team members did not display confidence in one another's reliability or dependability in terms of working with CLD families.

Respect

The interviews we conducted made it evident that respect is in the eye of the beholder. For the most part, the school-based personnel with whom we spoke (such as the school psychologist) felt that IEP team members—including families—regarded each other with esteem. Those who saw themselves more aligned with families than with the school (such as the ESOL teacher and the guidance counselor) felt that there was often an imbalance.

In sum, there were many areas of overlap between the themes presented by Blue-Banning et al. (2004) and the perspectives shared by the stakeholders we interviewed. However, as we continued to review our data, we realized that many of the themes we were seeing had less to do with stakeholders' perspectives on personal relationships and more to do with their perspectives on issues related to and stemming from the IEP process itself. In other words, we saw a shift in focus from people to procedures. This led us to revise our conceptual framework.

REVISING OUR CONCEPTUAL FRAMEWORK

We started this project with a focus on interpersonal dynamics as they relate to CLD families and IEP meetings. What emerged from our findings, however, was that participant experiences and recommendations focused more on the "big picture" of process and systems, which both influence and are influenced by the individuals involved.

For example, we heard quite a bit about communication among stakeholders, with a particular emphasis on the translator. The comments we heard were less about a translator's personal style or personality and more about how the system could be improved to ensure more effective translation during meetings in general. Table 12.1 summarizes our findings.

Table 12.1. Stakeholders, Suggestions, and Themes

Theme	Change school culture.	Change school culture.	Change school culture.	Improve meeting dynamics.	Improve meeting dynamics.	Improve meeting dynamics.	Increase awareness of SPED.	Increase awareness of SPED.	Increase awareness of SPED.
Specific suggestion	*Train teachers in CLD.*	*Encourage parent involvement.*	*Highlight importance of CLD / IEP.*	*Optimize logistics.*	*Mitigate "us vs. them."*	*Ensure understanding.*	*Train general education teachers in special education.*	*Train teachers in data collection.*	*Train translators in acronyms, law, etc.*
Principal	✓			✓	✓	✓		✓	✓
General Education Teacher	✓	✓		✓	✓	✓	✓	✓	✓
Special Education Teacher	✓	✓		✓	✓				
ESOL Teacher	✓	✓		✓	✓				✓
Advocate	✓		✓		✓				
Disability Rights Attorney	✓	✓	✓						
Parent	✓	✓			✓				
Translator	✓	✓		✓	✓	✓	✓		✓
School Psychologist	✓					✓			
Specialist	✓	✓	✓				✓	✓	
Transition Services Specialist			✓		✓				
Guidance Counselor	✓	✓			✓	✓			✓

When we asked participants for their suggestions for improvement, we saw three main themes being mentioned over and over during the interviews: the need for a change in school culture, the need for an increased awareness of special education, and the need for an improvement in IEP meeting dynamics. Figure 12.1 presents the three themes emerging from discussions; we created a revised conceptual framework for considering the experiences of CLD families with special education.

Change School Culture

The people we interviewed worked and lived in a variety of settings. We spoke with people working and living in rural, suburban, and urban areas, and we spoke with people in schools with highly affluent families and those working in schools with families of a low socioeconomic status. While their contexts were different, it is clear from our conversations that there needs to be a shift in school culture. With the sole exception of the principal, every person remarked that there needs to be a heightened awareness of cultural and linguistic diversity in their school building.

Underlying the suggestion for increased awareness is the assumption that increased awareness will in turn lead to increased understanding among all stakeholders. Whether or not this would automatically result in smoother or more effective IEP meetings is uncertain. However, there was general agreement that knowing more about the other people sitting at the table—especially in terms of their experiences, motivation, skills, and abilities—would be

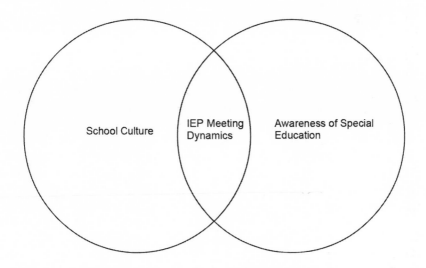

Figure 12.1.   Conceptual Framework 3: Systems Perspective

beneficial for improving communication among all stakeholders, developing more robust parental involvement, and promoting more receptive attitudes toward cultural and linguistic diversity.

Increase Awareness of Special Education

Another area about which the interviewees wanted to speak was that of special education. With the exception of the special education teacher and transition specialist, the school-based personnel had received little or no training in special education practices, law, or theory. A few remarked that they had "done" a workshop as part of a faculty meeting or professional development opportunity, but nothing more in-depth than that. Those who were not school-based (i.e., the parent and the advocate) described themselves as self-taught in these topics.

The lack of knowledge with regard to special education, particularly in terms of data collection, makes it difficult (at best) to imagine how IEP teams can meet the needs of a CLD student. This is especially true when the lack of understanding of special education is coupled with a lack of understanding about cultural and linguistic diversity. In these cases, it seems that many IEP teams rely heavily on the translator to be a "bridge" between the school-based personnel and the family.

Unfortunately, the translator's own lack of familiarity with acronyms, procedures, and other IEP-related matters often results in an overall breakdown in terms of communication. Thus, having all stakeholders work from a place of mutual understanding of the special education process would be beneficial from many different standpoints.

Improve IEP Meeting Dynamics

We see the IEP meeting as the place where attitudes about cultural and linguistic diversity and understanding of special education meet. The IEP table is where trust and respect are of the utmost importance, but also where the "us versus them" dynamic comes into play. Nearly everyone we interviewed agreed that the IEP meeting for a CLD student is something that schools could—and should—do better. The key is to be sure to involve parents more equitably and more often. By being flexible in terms of the meeting times, making sure parents understand what is happening, and ensuring a welcoming atmosphere, IEP meetings would be much more successful than the IEP team members currently think they are.

FINAL THOUGHTS

As we have conducted interviews, read over transcriptions, and crafted chapters, we have noticed that there is a common note running through all of the perspectives we have shared in the preceding chapters: uncertainty. This uncertainty manifests itself in virtually every aspect of an IEP meeting for a CLD student. Parents ask, "Can I trust the school?" Teachers ask, "Am I doing this right?" Administrators ask, "Do the parents understand?"

Given its highly procedure-oriented components, it can be hard to imagine that there is any ambiguity involved in creating an IEP. After all, there are checklists that must be checked and explanations that must be read aloud. The idea that there could be any question as to what should happen can—quite frankly—make one uneasy. That notion, taken along with the other themes we've discussed—the need for changing school culture, increasing awareness of special education, and improving IEP meeting dynamics—paints a bleak picture for the prospects of students who are dually identified.

In our interviews and our own experiences in schools, it is clear that many teachers are attempting to understand these issues, but we have also encountered many who do not seem able to do so. But here is where we also see some good news.

At no point during our interviews did anyone report anything other than a deep and abiding concern for CLD students and their welfare, both academically and non-academically. We were expecting that some might be dismissive or derogatory. Fortunately, that was not the case. With this in mind, we have several recommendations of our own to make.

MOVING FORWARD

One very sensible and feasible plan for schools seeking to improve the experiences of CLD families in special education is one that will also augment a school's professional culture and overall morale. This involves identifying, acknowledging, and learning from the in-house expertise of faculty and staff. Because one of the greatest areas of uncertainty exists across lines of specialization, staff development days could be dedicated to in-house presentations, rotating among special education, ESOL, and general education teachers. They could present key aspects related to their work with students and share methodologies for working with populations represented in classrooms.

Additionally, in terms of educating teachers in cultural competency and CLD populations, schools have access to a wealth of resources, starting with schools and families. A school with a parent outreach coordinator could ask that person to address cultures with which she is familiar, and to call upon a group of families willing to share key aspects of their cultures. Alternatively, teachers could create focus groups to explore the primary cultures represent-ed within their schools, proceeding from a spirit of inquiry as a way to understand aspects of these cultures and specifically how these impact views and experiences of schools and learning.

Because resources for schools are scarce and becoming scarcer, using in-house resources first allows school administrators to focus more narrowly on areas where no in-house expertise is available. This could include data col-lection, the use of assistive technologies, and other issues identified by teach-ers themselves as areas of greatest uncertainty for school staff in a particular building. These could be selected through a simple survey serving as a needs assessment. Absent funds for outside speakers, a district's own experts could address topics sequentially on professional development days and even in faculty meetings.

Regardless of how the issues we've shared in this book are addressed, our hope is that our framework will serve to raise awareness and to inform meaningful dialogue about serving students who are receiving special educa-tion services and are also culturally and linguistically diverse. In the intro-duction to this book, we shared a metaphor that many have used to express what it is like for parents of children with special needs to begin a journey to what can be a bewildering place, the IEP meeting table. With these perspec-tives, stakeholders can guide each other in the interest of achieving the best possible outcome for students, so that those students can maximize their potential in their school years and throughout their lives. This, after all, is at the core of our collective educational mission.

Appendix

Commonly Used Acronyms

AYP: Adequate Yearly Progress
CST: Child Study Team
ED: Emotional Disturbance
EI: Early Intervention
ESL: English as a Second Language
ESOL: English for Speakers of Other Languages
ESY: Extended School Year
FAPE: Free and Appropriate Public Education
FBA: Functional Behavioral Assessment
IDEA: Individuals with Disabilities Education Act
IEP: Individualized Education Program
LD: Learning Disability
LEA: Local Education Agency
LRE: Least Restrictive Environment
OT: Occupational Therapy
PLOP: Present Level of Performance
PT: Physical Therapy
S/LP: Speech/Language Pathology

NOTE

A full list of acronyms can be found at http://www.parentcenterhub.org/acronyms/.

References

Arizona Ombudsman (2016). *Special education dispute resolution.* Retrieved from http://www. azed.gov/disputeresolution/2016/06/23/iep/

Avramidis, E., Bayliss, P., & Burden, R. (2000). A survey into mainstream teachers' attitudes towards the inclusion of children with special educational needs in the ordinary school in one local education authority. *Educational Psychology, 20*(2), 191–211. https://doi.org/10. 1080/713663717

Banks, J. A. (2001). Multicultural education programs evaluation checklist. In J. Banks (Ed.), *Cultural diversity and education* (4th ed.) (pp. 336–344). Boston: Allyn & Bacon.

Blue-Banning, M., Summers, A., Frankland, H. C., Nelson, L. L., & Beegle, G. (2004). Dimensions of family and professional partnerships: Constructive guidelines for collaboration. *Exceptional Children, 70,* 167–184.

Caskey, M. M., & Carpenter, J. (2014). Building teacher collaboration school-wide. *AMLE Magazine.* Retrieved from https://www.amle.org/BrowsebyTopic/WhatsNew/WNDet/ TabId/270/ArtMID/888/ArticleID/446/Building-Teacher-Collaboration-School-wide.aspx

Cartledge, G., Lo, Y-Y., Vincent, C. G., & Robinson-Ervin, P. (2015). Culturally responsive classroom management. In E. T. Emmer & E. J. Sabornie (Eds.), *Handbook of Classroom Management* (pp. 411–430). New York: Routledge.

Chiariello, E. (2014). Old problem, new approach. *Teaching Tolerance.* Retrieved from https:// www.tolerance.org/magazine/old-problem-new-approach

Collier, V. (1995). *Promoting academic success for ESL students: Understanding second language acquisition at school.* Jersey City, NJ: New Jersey Teachers of English to Speakers of Other Languages.

Colorado Department of Education, Office of Special Education. (2015). Cultural mediators, translators, and interpreters. Retrieved from http://www.cde.state.co.us/cdesped/ta_ culturalmediators

Czop Assaf, L., Garza, R., & Battle, J. (2010). Multicultural teacher education: Examining the perceptions, practices, and coherence in one teacher preparation program. *Teacher Education Quarterly,* 115–135.

Dalien, S. (2014). *Teachers' role in an IEP meeting.* Special Ed Resource. Retrieved from https://specialedresource.com/teachers-role-iep-meeting

Deal, T. E., & Peterson, K. D. (2016). *Shaping school culture.* San Francisco: Jossey-Bass.

District of Colombia Public Schools. (2011). *Roles and responsibilities.* Retrieved from http:// www.schoolspecialty.com/ssi-wdf-ucm/webContent/groups/public/@guestmktger/ documents/webcontent/x023653.pdf

European Agency for Development in Special Needs Education. (2010). *Teacher Education for Inclusion*. Retrieved from https://www.european-agency.org/sites/default/files/TE4I-Literature-Review.pdf

Fellin, M., Desmarais, C., & Lindsay, S. (2014). An examination of clinicians' experiences of collaborative culturally competent service delivery to immigrant families raising a child with a physical disability. *Disability and Rehabilitation, 37,* 1961–1969. https://10.3109/09638288.2014.993434

Fleischman, D., & Imaz-Marial, O. (2015). Going "old school": From bedside manner to deskside manner. *Student Success, 6,* 81–86.

Gershenson, S., Holt, S. B., & Papageorge, N. (2016). Who believes in me? The effect of student-teacher demographic match on teacher expectations. *The Economics of Education Review, 52,* 209–224. https://doi.org/10.1016/j.econedurev.2016.03.002

Good, M. E., Masewicz, S., & Vogel, L. (2010). Latino English language learners: Bridging achievement and cultural gaps between schools and families. *Journal of Latinos and Education, 9*(4), 321–339. doi:10.1080/15348431.2010.491048

Grafwallner, P. (2017). What I've learned from special ed teachers. *Edutopia.* Retrieved from https://www.edutopia.org/article/what-ive-learned-special-ed-teachers

Higgins, J. (2016). Schools don't talk clearly to us, immigrant parents say. *Seattle Times*, April 19. Retrieved fromhttps://www.seattletimes.com/seattle-news/education/immigrant-parents-say-language-gap-hampers-their-involvement-in-kids-education/

Ikkanda, Z. (n.d.) *Data data data.* Retrieved from http://www.specialeducationadvisor.com/data-data-data/

Johnson, B. (2011). Making the most out of teacher collaboration. *Edutopia.* Retrieved from https://www.edutopia.org/blog/teacher-collaboration-strategies-ben-johnson

Lima, A. H. (2000). Voices from the basement: Breaking through the pedagogy of indifference. In Z. F. Beykont (Ed.), *Lifting every voice: Pedagogy and politics of bilingualism* (pp. 221–232). Cambridge, MA: Harvard Education Publishing Group.

Marquez Chisholm, I. (1994). Preparing teachers for multicultural classrooms. *Journal of Educational Issues of Language Minority Students, 14,* 43–68. Retrieved from http://www.edtechpolicy.org/ArchivedWebsites/chisholm.htm

Maxwell, L. A. (2014). U.S. school enrollment hits majority-minority milestone. *Education Week, 34*(1), 12, 14–15.

Mazzotti, V. L., & Rowe, D. A. (2015). Meeting the transition needs of students with disabilities in the 21st century. *Teaching Exceptional Children, 47,* 298–300. http://doi.org/10.1177/0040059915587695

McElhinny, K. T., & Pellegrin, D. R. (2014). The principal's role with IEP teams. *Communicator, 38*(2). Retrieved from https://www.naesp.org/communicator-october-2014/principal-s-role-iep-teams

Minnesota Department of Education. (2005). *The ELL companion to reducing bias in special education evaluation*. Retrieved from http://www.asec.net/Archives/Manuals/ELL%20companion%20Manual%20020212%5B1%5D.pdf

Montelungo, A. (2014). Latino parents' perceptions of IEP meetings. *McNair Scholars Journal, 16,* 109–131.

Mulligan, E. (2011). *The facts on charter schools and students with disabilities.* Retrieved from http://www.parentcenterhub.org/charters/

National Center for Education Statistics (NCES). (2017a). *English language learners in U.S. schools.* Retrieved from https://nces.ed.gov/programs/coe/indicator_cgf.asp

National Center for Education Statistics (NCES). (2017b). *Racial/ethnic enrollment in public schools.* Retrieved from https://nces.ed.gov/programs/coe/indicator_cge.asp

National Education Association. (2000). *Diversity toolkit.* Retrieved from http://www.nea.org/tools/diversity-toolkit.html

No Child Left Behind Act of 2001, P.L. 107-110, 20 U.S.C. § 6319. (2002).

Park, Y., & Thomas, R. (2012). Educating English-language learners with special needs: Beyond cultural and linguistic considerations. *Journal of Education and Practice, 3*(9), 52–58.

Plain Writing Act of 2010, 5 USC 105, P.L. 111-274. (2010). Retrieved from https://www.gpo.gov/fdsys/pkg/PLAW-111publ274/pdf/PLAW-111publ274.pdf

Rim, L. R., & Kothari, S. (2018). *Key trends in special education in charter schools: A secondary analysis of the civil rights data collection.* Retrieved from https://static1. squarespace.com/.../280272+NCSECS+Full+Report_WEB+%281%29.pdf

Rossetti, Z., Sauer, J. S., Bui, O., & Ou, S. (2018). Developing collaborative partnerships with culturally and linguistically diverse families during the IEP process. *Teaching Exceptional Children, 50,* 172–182. https://doi.org/10.1177/0040059918758163

Shafer, L. (2017). *How to have a successful IEP meeting.* Retrieved from https://www.gse. harvard.edu/news/uk/17/09/how-have-successful-iep-meeting

Sharma, U., Forlin, C., & Loreman, T. (2008). Impact of training on pre-service teachers' attitudes and concerns about inclusive education and sentiments about persons with disabilities. *Disability & Society, 23*(7), 773–785. https://doi.org/10.1080/09687590802469271

Sleeter, C. E. (2016). Critical race theory and the whiteness of teacher education. *Urban Education, 52*(2), 155–169. https://doi.org/10.1177/0042085916668957

Trainor, A., Murray, A., & Kim, H-J. (2016). English learners with disabilities in high school: Population characteristics, transition programs, and postschool outcomes. *Remedial and Special Education, 37,* 146–158. https://doi.org/10.1177/0741932515626797

U.S. Department of Education, Office of Special Education Programs (OSEP). (2014). *White House initiative on educational excellence for Hispanic families and special education.* Retrieved from https://sites.ed.gov/hispanic-initiative/files/2014/06/Webinar-Hispanic-Families-and-Special-Education_June-2014.pdf

U.S. Department of Education, Office of Special Education Programs (OSEP). (2016). IEP translation: Communication from OSEP regarding the government's statement of interest in R. vs. The School District of Philadelphia. Retrieved from https://www2.ed.gov/policy/speced/guid/idea/memosdcltrs/iep-translation-06-14-2016.pdf

U.S. Department of Education. (2018). Tools and Resources for Addressing English Learners with Disabilities. Chapter 6 in *English Learner Tool Kit.* Retrieved from https://www2.ed. gov/about/offices/list/oela/english-learner-toolkit/chap6.pdf

Villegas, A. M., & Lucas, T. (2002). *Educating culturally responsive teachers: A coherent approach.* Albany: State University of New York Press.

Vilson, J. (2015). Empowering educators through cultural competence. *Edutopia.* Retrieved from https://www.edutopia.org/blog/empowering-educators-through-cultural-competence-jose-vilson

Zamora, G. (2015). *Participation of Latino Spanish-speaking families in the IEP process.* Retrieved from https://digitalcommons.csumb.edu/cgi/viewcontent.cgi?article=1517& context

About the Authors

Karrin Lukacs is an award-winning associate professor of curriculum and instruction at Shenandoah University in Winchester, Virginia, where she teaches (or has taught) classroom management, program evaluation, and assessment (to name a few). Her research interests are eclectic and, as a result, she has published work on a variety of topics, including teacher change agency, online learning, and stay-at-home mothers who want to become teachers. She holds a PhD in education from George Mason University and holds a Mindful Educator certificate. As an Apple Distinguished Educator, she is an avid proponent of educational technology and its possibilities for both K–12 and postsecondary classrooms. In her free time, she enjoys spending time with her family, serving on several advisory boards, and thinking about what her next project will be.

Sherry L. Steeley is an associate teaching professor at Georgetown University in Washington, DC, where she teaches in a program for preparing ESL/EFL teachers and participates in international teacher training programs. She has worked and conducted research with teachers from the United States, China, Korea, Pakistan, Spain, the Republic of Georgia, Peru, Panama, as well as various groups of visiting international teachers. She holds a PhD in education from George Mason University, a Certificate in Autism Spectrum Disorders from Virginia Commonwealth University, and an MA in international economics and Latin American studies from Johns Hopkins School of Advanced International Studies. In her free time, she enjoys spending time outdoors, hiking, and exploring the world with her son and other family and friends. She is perpetually considering educational and sociocultural improvement.

Made in the USA
Middletown, DE
01 April 2021